TEACHING BY HEART

The Foxfire Interviews

TEACHING BY HEART

The Foxfire Interviews

SARA DAY HATTON

Teachers College, Columbia University
New York and London

Published by Teachers College Press, 1234 Amsterdam Avenue, New York, NY 10027

Library of Congress Cataloging-in-Publication Data

Hatton, Sara Day.
    Teaching by heart : the Foxfire interviews / Sara Day Hatton.
        p. cm.
    ISBN 0-8077-4539-1 (cloth : alk. paper) — ISBN 0-8077-4538-3 (pbk. : alk. paper)
        1. Effective teaching—United States.   2. Teachers—United States—
    Attitudes—Interviews.   3. Education—United States—Philosophy.
    4. Active learning—United States.   I. Foxfire Fund.   II. Title.
    LB1025.3.H39 2005
    371.39—dc22   2004058003

ISBN 0-8077-4538-3 (paper)
ISBN 0-8077-4539-1 (cloth)

Printed on acid-free paper
Manufactured in the United States of America

12 11 10 09 08 07 06 05   8 7 6 5 4 3 2 1

To all teachers who continue to pursue something none of us has caught yet: May you find joy in the search;

To the many teachers who came through the Foxfire "door" in that pursuit;

To Bobby Starnes and Christy Stevens, in abiding friendship and love;

To Poppy, "Sister" says it all;

And to David, always.

—Sara Day Hatton

Foxfire is a not-for-profit, educational, and literary organization based in Rabun County, Georgia. Foxfire's learner-centered, community-based educational approach is advocated through both a regional demonstration site grounded in the Southern Appalachian culture that gave rise to Foxfire, and a national program of teacher training and support that promotes a sense of place and appreciation of local people, community, and culture as essential educational tools.

For information about Foxfire, contact:

Ann Moore, President

The Foxfire Fund, Inc.

P.O. Box 541

Mountain City, GA 30562-0541

(706) 746-5828 phone

(706) 746-5829 fax

foxfire@foxfire.org

www.foxfire.org

Contents

PART III—The Teacher as Moral and Philosophical Guide

PART IV—Teaching Place, Fostering Consequential Learning

PART V—Teaching and Educational Change

PART VI—Reflections on Powerful Conversations

Acknowledgments

This book grew out of collaborative thinking and the advice and suggestions of a number of people.

The original interviews were published in *The Active Learner: A Foxfire Journal for Teachers*, of which I was editor for 5 years. The content for each issue evolved from extensive conversations among Foxfire staff members and discussions with teacher-members. Of course, whom to choose for interview subjects was an important part of these discussions. These talks centered on educators that teachers admired and with whom they would have liked to talk about the practice of teaching. I am indebted to Bobby Ann Starnes and the teachers for their insightful suggestions.

I am also grateful to Bobby and all the Foxfire staff for creating an environment of encouragement and support that nurtured the idea of writing a book based on the interviews. Significantly, I want to thank current Foxfire President, Ann Moore, and the Foxfire Board of Directors for their unflagging support in seeing the book through to publication.

My appreciation also goes to Christy Stevens, former Director of Teacher Support at Foxfire, who served as a sounding board for the edited interviews.

I am also indebted to two people at Teachers College Press: Brian Ellerbeck for his belief in the book and his support through the publication process, and Wendy Schwartz, my editor, for her valuable input.

It is particularly important to acknowledge that two of the interviews were done before I joined the Foxfire staff. Lacy Hunter, then a senior at Rabun County High School and a member of *The Foxfire Magazine* staff, did an excellent job interviewing Maxine Greene. Elaine Minton, who briefly served as editor of the Journal, conducted and wrote the engaging interview with Ted Sizer.

Finally, I want to thank the wonderful educators who were interviewed for this book. Throughout the interview process and the writing of this book, they strove to reflect on their lives and to convey their thinking in a desire to connect with teachers.

To all these people, I extend heartfelt gratitude for helping to make this book possible.

—Sara Day Hatton

TEACHING BY HEART

The Foxfire Interviews

Introduction

Teaching is one of the most challenging professions a person can face. Ask anyone who has walked into a classroom for the first time, armed with only 4 years of college and a love of children, teaching, and learning. Ask anyone who has been teaching for 20 or more years.

Better yet, ask the people who are interviewed in this book, some of the most revered people in education. These are people who think deeply about teaching and learning and communicate their thinking in ways that influence educational thought. Through this thinking and the process of reflection, they all have come to know that teaching will remain a challenge to them throughout their lives. In the following chapters, they generously and frankly reflect on and share with us the challenges they have faced in their teaching practices and careers.

This book is divided into six Parts: Part I, Becoming a Teacher; Part II, Teaching and the Power of Story; Part III, The Teacher as Moral and Philosophical Guide; Part IV, Teaching Place, Fostering Consequential Learning; Part V, Teaching and Educational Change; and Part VI, Reflections on Powerful Conversations.

Each part reflects the primary focus of the interviews contained within it. However, it must be said that the topics covered in each interview range farther than these simple classifications can convey. On reading, it becomes clear that the interview subjects relate experiences or reflections that add to or resonate with interviews in other parts. This serves to make the interviews richer as a whole.

Also, in the tradition of Foxfire and offering choice, each interview subject was asked if he or she would like to include a small bit of personal information in the biographical sketch at the beginning of each interview. You will note that some provided interesting facts about personal interests, some chose to include information about their families, and some chose to leave personal information out. We respect their choices.

The interviews originally were conducted for *The Active Learner: A Foxfire Journal for Teachers*. As stated in the Acknowledgments, two were done before I joined the Foxfire staff. Lacy Hunter, then a senior at Rabun

County High School and a student editor of *The Foxfire Magazine*, served as guest interviewer of Maxine Greene. Elaine Minton interviewed Ted Sizer during her brief but productive time as editor of the Journal in early 1996. I conducted the remaining interviews over a period of 5 years from 1996 through 2001 while editor of the Journal and Director of Communications at Foxfire.

For 6 years, *The Active Learner*, now out of publication, was the primary avenue of communication for and about the educational approach of Foxfire, an organization working to promote educational change through the Foxfire Approach to Teaching and Learning.

Foxfire's work is built on the belief that the experiences of teachers and students are very valuable and provide the base on which to build spiraling, meaningful learning. Through reflection and wrestling with ideas, teachers and students gain insight into what they have learned and an understanding of why it is important.

Foxfire began in 1966 when Eliot Wigginton, a teacher struggling to reach his students in a rural Appalachian school, gave up and asked them to find their own ways to learn the English they were expected to master.

The students chose to interview the people they knew in the community and to gather and write stories of local history and folkways. They wanted to put the stories and articles together and publish a magazine, which they chose to name *Foxfire*.

Excitement was high as the students took charge of their own learning. Over time, the students, in what came to be known as the Foxfire Class in Rabun County, Georgia, gained a strong sense of their abilities in interviewing, writing, editing, photography, and publishing. They also became documenters of both their community and a vanishing way of life. Importantly, they also developed an abiding sense of commitment to their community.

Eventually, the interviews and articles written by the Foxfire students were compiled into *The Foxfire Book* series; astonishingly, the books found a national audience. The series has sold over 8 million copies, quite an affirmation of student struggle and work.

The success of the books made it possible to found The Foxfire Fund, Inc., and led to the development of the Foxfire Approach to Teaching and Learning.

Teachers who use the Foxfire Approach are guided by 11 Core Practices. Through implementation of the Core Practices, they create classrooms in which all work is active, learner-centered, and community-focused. In these classrooms, learning grows out of student interests. Most significantly, all student work must be academically sound, meaningful in the lives of the students, and tied directly to the school's mandated curriculum, and must meet high levels of academic expectations.

Many teachers were drawn to use writing projects to inspire their own students, yet few of these efforts succeeded. At first the Foxfire staff members were puzzled by this lack of success. They—and Foxfire students—had conducted presentations across the country on how Foxfire had taken root. But, in time, they realized that the teachers who tried to recreate Foxfire's experience failed to understand the underlying concept behind the magazine—student choice and academic integrity. The teachers didn't grasp that student decision-making was at the heart of the creation of *The Foxfire Magazine*. The students solved the challenges and problems that arose from publishing a magazine: They chose whom they would interview, they took the photographs, they edited their own work, they determined the merit of articles to be published, and they raised the funds for the publication. They chose what and how they would learn, and that experience engaged them in learning that was meaningful and exciting to them.

While they knew what was at the heart of the work of the Foxfire Class, staff members wanted to find a way to express what actually happens *in* a Foxfire class. They sought to understand it better themselves and to find the words to convey how this work could be implemented in other school settings.

Over the next 35 years, Foxfire staff members, in collaboration with interested teachers, developed a set of ideas that in combination are called the Foxfire Approach to Teaching and Learning (to learn more about the Foxfire Approach, visit the Foxfire website at www.foxfire.org). Through this approach, teacher practitioners can develop ways to engage their students in active learning characterized by student choice and decision-making. At the very center of encouraging students to choose and make decisions is an understanding of the value of personal experience.

This appreciation for understanding that is developed through practice and reflection underlies all of Foxfire's work with teachers. Through personal contact and its publications, Foxfire encourages teachers to reflect on their experiences in the classroom and to share their stories about their practices.

When *The Active Learner* was conceptualized by former Foxfire president Bobby Ann Starnes, she saw the publication as a tool to support the practice of teaching. From the beginning, teacher classroom experiences were to be the primary component of the Journal.

With this established, Starnes asked teachers what else they thought the Journal should include. Almost all said they wanted interviews with educational leaders whose work had informed their practices. Many of them suggested whom they thought we should interview, and we included their ideas among those we contacted to request interviews.

For the next 6 years the interviews in the Journal provided insight into the thinking of educators who have made a difference in the way we all perceive teaching and learning. Then in 2001, we decided to reach out to a broader audience with the interviews, and the idea for *Teaching by Heart: The Foxfire Interviews* was born.

So carrying on in the tradition of Foxfire, we offer this book to inspire, reassure, comfort, confound, annoy, and perhaps guide you to new levels of your thinking. We believe that's important. But in the final analysis, it is the significance you find in these stories to shape your own thinking that matters—both in your life and in the lives of your students.

Chapter One

Creating Interviews
That Speak to Teachers

Introduction

Doing an interview is like taking a trip with a road map. You may have basic knowledge about the road ahead, a bit of information about the towns you will pass through. Yet even with all your preparations, you can never really know what you will find until you travel down that road, making excursions into towns along the way.

So it has been in interviewing the subjects included in this book. All are prominent figures in education, people who have spent their lives practicing, reflecting, and theorizing about the hard work of teaching and its greater implications for our world. Like you, I was familiar with them and their work; but although that knowledge gave me some insight, it did not prepare me for what I found when talking with them. Their responses to questions went beyond what they think to *how* they think, revealing the processes through which they went to become some of the most influential people in the field. Additionally, they displayed a generous willingness to share their very human struggles—struggles that many of you will recognize as similar to your own.

Choosing the Interview Questions

I believe these interviews are like no others you will read—not because of the interviewer's skills but because of the way the interviews were envisioned and for *whom* they were envisioned.

Of course, there have been many earlier interviews with Robert Coles, Maxine Greene, Alfie Kohn, Vivian Paley, Eleanor Duckworth, Ted Sizer, and others included here. In most, these educators discussed their philosophy of education, their books, their methods, and their ideas for educational reform.

However, when the Foxfire staff asked teachers what they wanted from the planned interviews, they asked for something more. They wanted to get to know these educators as people, as teachers. The teachers wanted to know whether these influential educators had struggled with the issues they themselves were struggling with and what in their experience and thinking had guided them. The teachers wanted to see into the educators' thinking. In effect, they wanted to demystify the experts and see them as people who, like themselves, were still grappling with becoming all they could be as professional educators.

With this in mind, we knew the interviews would focus primarily on the interview subjects' experiences in the classroom, their response to what they saw taking place in classrooms, and the meaning they took from those experiences to inform their own work. Therefore, the interviews focused on what the subjects could tell us about their experiences that would impact teachers' thinking and practice or cause readers to think differently about themselves and their profession. Most important, we wanted each interview to give teachers the sense that they themselves might have sat down with the interview subject and asked the questions closest to their hearts. We wanted readers to come away with the understanding that these renowned people grapple with the same issues teachers struggle with every day—that both they and our readers are engaged in what we see as the endless process of becoming a teacher.

The Same but Different

We then began to think of whom we should interview and how to structure the interviews. Foxfire teacher-members came through as a resource in this step of the planning also. They were asked: If you could talk with an educator and ask her or him questions, who would that person be? What would you want to ask? Their suggestions were woven into our concept for the interviews and, after much thought and many revisions, we devised a list of classic questions to ask each of the interviewees. The questions were shaped to evoke personal reflections on the interviewees' experiences inside the classroom and/or their thinking about teaching and what goes on in the classroom. For example, we asked each to tell us about a memorable learning experience, the struggles they faced as teachers, how they worked their way through the challenges they faced, and the ways those experiences influence their work today.

At first I was excited about the questions we had formulated. They got to the heart of what teachers wanted to know about these people. Then as my first interviews approached, I had doubts about using the same basic questions. What if they all answered similarly? What if the questions evoked uninteresting or superficial answers? What if those interviewed could not relate to the more personal tone we wanted to establish?

I soon found I had no reason to worry; it was quickly obvious that the questions could stay generally the same. The answers given by these fascinating people were riveting and enlightening and revealed the very real humanness of those often-revered educators. After the completion of a number of interviews, it also became obvious that, in fact, the use of the same questions made comparing and contrasting the answers all the more interesting. The similarity of the questions resulted in richer, more meaningful understandings for readers and provoked reflective thought and critical analysis. Also, no two people gave similar answers.

In addition, the interviews revealingly supported a very important idea in Foxfire's work: the same but different. As we work with teachers, we encourage them to find colleagues whose work is constructed on many of the same values and beliefs they themselves hold. We also emphasize that it's important to honor the differences in how those values and beliefs are applied, as a result of contrasting personalities, backgrounds, and experiences.

It was apparent that, like the teachers we work with, those interviewed had been shaped by very different experiences. It was also apparent that the practical applications of their shared values were played out in wonderfully diverse ways.

For example, when asked to relate a memorable learning experience and its impact on her work, Yetta Goodman recalled the moment when, although she was perceived to be an excellent teacher, "it dawned on me that I was a performer and not a teacher. . . . I then began to see that I needed to showcase the kids, not have them thinking I was the center of attention."

In contrast, Eleanor Duckworth says, "Our teacher read us a play that we were going to produce and asked us what we thought would be a good name for this play. It was so simple; that's all it was. And I knew exactly what should be the name of my play and I waved my hand and waved my hand. . . . it felt wonderful to have chosen the name of a play. . . . That's what drives my work—trying to engage learners with their own ideas."

Why Write a Book and Why This Book?

Over 6 years, the interviews grew in number and finally constituted a collection of very thought-provoking material. We believed it deserved a wider readership than our Journal subscribers. We wanted teachers and other educators outside the Foxfire membership to have access to the information contained in the interviews, and I wanted to put them in perspective as a whole. Both the staff and I were convinced that publication of the interviews in book form, with supporting chapters, was a natural progression for the materials.

Overlapping Themes

Each reader will take from the interviews the meanings that are most appropriate for their own thinking, development, and interests. These meanings will be integrated into their thinking and practice in ways unique to their teaching sites, challenges, and opportunities.

However, as the interviews are read, it's important to note certain threads that run through them. For example, every interview subject talks about the importance of teachers reflecting on their work in order to take risks in their classrooms, improve their thinking and practice, and grow as educators. In illustration of that advice, the interviews themselves became a forum for these educators to reflect on practice and their own professional development. They reflected on their experiences as learners and as educators. They shared the theoretical frameworks that inform their practice and explored how those ideas grew out of these experiences. What emerges is a series of interviews that serve as rich examples of the value and rewards of taking time to reflect on teaching and learning. The interviews make clear that we must hold dear the sense we make of our experiences and how they relate to our beliefs, values, and life missions.

Those interviewed talked at length about the importance of teachers networking and building support systems of like-minded colleagues. Many clearly see fellow educators as an important resource to keep teachers grounded in their ideas and as a resource for support through the unsettling process of change. These interviews contribute to that resource of support in that they contain advice, examples, strategies, and experiences. Interestingly, the interviews also represent the efforts of those interviewed to both be and feel part of a collegial community of educators.

The content of the interviews also speaks to a need for all teachers to seek out people with whom they can share their frustrations, ideas, and dreams about teaching and learning. "If someone is inclined to take a chance and do something different—not just adding some new technique like getting kids on the internet but really rethinking the whole philosophy of learning—they shouldn't try to do it alone," Alfie Kohn says. "They should, at the very least, find a colleague to supply moral support and new ideas to help them avoid being burned out and depressed." The interview subjects' common grounding in progressive education results in a grouping of educators whose ideas are, in many ways, mutually supportive.

Exploring Contrasting Views and Styles

However, it is also helpful to acknowledge the points at which the interviewees' experiences and ideas diverge, leaving the reader to use her or his discretion when considering the advice, suggested strategies, and different approaches addressed in this book. Further, each person interviewed has a different way of talking about his or her work. For example, Ira Shor is firmly based in a philosophical and theoretical framework when discussing his ideas. On the other hand, both Bobby Ann Starnes and Jack Shelton talk about their ideas within the context of practice, focusing on the tangible ways in which their ideas and beliefs take form. Different from both of these is Yetta Goodman's interview, which is also full of ideas and reflections but is distinguished by her marked use of personal narrative or the telling of life experiences that led her to form her teaching theories.

The contrasting conversational styles actually work to reinforce many of the ideas explored in this book. The interviews are characterized by an engaging interplay of personal experience and theoretical ideas. Some of the personal narratives shared by those interviewed work really well when considered in relationship to theories put forth by other interviewees. Yetta Goodman's memory of accompanying her non-English-speaking mother to school to ask the teacher why she received a "D" in art class humanizes much of Alfie Kohn's theories about the demoralizing effect grades can have on learners of all ages.

Also noteworthy is Donald Graves's memory of trying to work through the death of his friend in the Korean War within the context of writing about *War and Peace* for a literature class. Its prominence lies not only in the way it inspires empathy in the reader, but also in the way it illustrates what many of the interview subjects touched on in a philosophical way: the importance of knowing your students and respecting their experiences. It personalizes Eleanor Duckworth's advice to teachers to "pay attention to the sense . . . students are making of whatever they are doing. If you don't understand them, keep probing until you see the sense."

Taking Risks, Rethinking Our Practices

All the interview subjects reveal the great value in being risk-takers. These are people who think deeply about their practice and are willing to make significant changes in their thinking and in their work. Vivian Paley recalls an early realization in the classroom that led her to change her practice in a way that eventually led to her career as an acclaimed writer.

> I was certainly an adequate teacher, but . . . for a long time I was mimicking things I remembered. . . . Then I began to seek a way that the passion in the children's play could be transferred to a passion for school, that connections could be made between their play and their *learning.*

When studied, the experiences recalled by the interview subjects are powerful because they can inspire us to rethink our own actions and assumptions about our practices. And in so doing, we hope the interviews serve to fulfill the ultimate intent of the men and women in this book: to improve schools for children. While each person interviewed goes about working toward change in an essentially unique way, their dreams and aspirations for teachers and children are similar. To this end, they support democratic classrooms and believe in the strength, the integrity, and the wisdom of teachers to make the right choices for their students.

What's Missing?

There is another point that must be made about the interviews—they reveal something about the very culture of educational hierarchy today. Cultural and economic diversity is apparent. For example, Yetta Goodman is "a bilingual kid from a poor family in an urban area"; Bobby Ann Starnes describes herself as a "hillbilly" whose family migrated out of the mountains and into an urban setting; and Ira Shor grew up in a working-class family in the South Bronx. Still, as the interviews developed over the period of 4 years, we realized they are primarily the stories of White, middle-class men and women. This reflects a disturbing reality of power systems in the United States. However, as these interviews are read, it will become apparent that these exceptional people who are making powerful contributions to our educational system have, write about, and champion ideas and beliefs to broaden that system to include and celebrate the richness of diverse voices, understandings, and values.

Being Part of a Continuum of Thinkers

Of course, interviews with powerful people who have shaped and inspired the thinking of two generations of teachers are worthwhile and intriguing to read. These men and women are the heirs of such notable theorists and thinkers as John Dewey, Jean Piaget, Anna Freud, Erik

Erikson, Paulo Freire, and others. Aware of their own remarkable influence on educational thought today, we have attempted through these interviews to find how these outstanding educators evolved. "Hearing" them speak about how they were inspired and challenged, the issues with which they struggled, and how they worked through those struggles, can add to our understanding of the process of creative and cognitive growth for all of us.

We hope you will study and reflect on the experiences and the wisdom gained by these remarkable men and women, that you will come back to the book again and again over time, that you will take these experiences "to heart," as Robert Coles says, and that you will find yourselves a little uncomfortable with some of the thoughts expressed in the book but recognize that this is a good place to be. Or, as Alfie Kohn describes it, "The people who look stricken and gulp are the people whose classroom I want my kid in because they have the gumption to try to get better at what they do." We hope that by uncovering the struggle of "the experts," you will be encouraged to find and nourish your own seeds of power.

So, as you read the following interviews, we hope you, too, will have, as Parker Palmer calls it, "an alchemy of heart," and find fuel for moving your thinking and your teaching practice to higher levels.

BECOMING A TEACHER

The interviews in Part I were chosen because they speak eloquently of the experiences that molded the professional lives of the interview subjects.

Chapter Two

ELEANOR DUCKWORTH

Engaging Learners with Their Own Ideas

Eleanor Duckworth, professor at Harvard University and a former student, colleague, and translator of Jean Piaget, grounds her work in Piaget's theories of the nature and development of intelligence. Her interest, however, is in teaching and the experience of teachers and learners of all ages, both in and out of school. She has worked on curriculum development, teacher education, and program evaluation in the United States, Switzerland, Africa, and her native Canada.

Before entering teaching at the university level, Duckworth taught third grade and was an elementary school science curriculum developer. She was Senior Research Associate and Founding Director of the Lighthouse Learning Program at the Atlantic Institute on Education in Halifax, Nova Scotia.

Her publications include: *"Tell Me More": Listening to Learners Explain* (2001), *Teacher to Teacher* (with The Experienced Teachers Group, 1997), *The Having of Wonderful Ideas and Other Essays on Teaching and Learning* (1987, winner of the 1988 AERA award for outstanding research contribution in the areas of teaching and teacher education), and *Science Education: A Minds-on Approach for the Elementary Years* (1990).

Duckworth lives in Cambridge, Massachusetts, and is a modern dancer performing with the Back Porch Dance Company.

Interview—Winter 1999

SH: At Foxfire we believe teachers' memorable learning experiences and thinking about them can inform our own teaching practice. Can you tell us about one of your memorable learning experiences?

ED: In all of my formal schooling, I have only three memorable learning experiences. And they were all where I was called upon to have some ideas of my own. One was in grade 3 when our teacher read us a play that we were going to produce and asked us what we thought would be a good name for this play. It was so simple; that's all it was. And I knew exactly what should be the name of my play, and I waved my hand and waved my hand. I don't know how many she asked but I believe we all said the same thing. Nonetheless, it felt wonderful to have chosen the name of a play. I think she must have known that it was pretty obvious what we would choose. But it still felt terrific.

Another time was in grade 8 in geometry class when we already knew how to find the area of a triangle and of a rectangle and the teacher asked us to invent ways of finding the area of an octagon. I found that totally enthralling and came up with lots of ways.

The third was in my freshman year in college in a biology class where I had an assignment without a specific question. I was simply to look at the bones of the leg of a horse and of a member of the cat family. And just by myself having to compare the leg bones of these two different animals and then with what I knew about my own bones was truly amazing.

All these were examples of times when teachers gave me the opportunity to think on my own.

SH: Can you also tell us about learning experiences you had as a teacher?

ED: I was thrown into elementary science curriculum development not from having been a teacher but because of having studied with Piaget. During this work, I was starting to learn how to be a teacher. I was doing a little pilot teaching then, and I was trying to prepare for my next class. So I found someone who was not a scientist to try out my next activities. I wanted to bring him up to where the kids were by now. I carefully did the first experiment and he got through that and came to the conclusion I wanted. I carefully went through the second one, and again, he came to the conclusion I wanted, and that set up the third one. I thought he'd be ready to see exactly what I wanted him to see, but he made some comment about the role of weight in this prediction. Now this insight had been involved in one of the first two experiments I'd had him do. So I exclaimed, "But you just *did* weight!" Because if he'd really understood what I thought he had by then understood, he wouldn't have brought weight into this particular problem.

So I learned something that I already *knew* as a psychologist with kids but it really wasn't a part of me—you can't assume people have understood something because you've led them through it very carefully. Nowadays that is absolutely critical to everything I do.

SH: Would you describe your role as a teacher and how did you discover it?

ED: I think a teacher should get people interested in the subject matter by putting them in direct contact with the subject matter, not through somebody else's words about it but right in contact with the subject matter. Then the teacher should listen. That is, just listen to what the students think. Encourage them to keep thinking, and keep them thinking about the subject matter by bringing in new angles. Taking them through *my* sequence fails on two counts—one, it's boring to the learner; and two, it doesn't correspond to the ways *their* minds are taking on the subject. So it misses the boat.

So keep them thinking about the subject matter, listen to what they say, and don't explain it—let them explain it to you, to themselves, and to each other. That's what I think.

How I came to that is a long story. It wasn't until I had the chance to learn that way that I realized the potential of my own mind. As long as I was trying to understand what someone was explaining to me, I kept thinking that none of those ideas were mine, they were somebody else's and my job was to try to understand somebody else's ideas. But as soon as it was put into my hands to be the one doing the explaining, then I started to think I had some pretty good ideas also.

SH: In your efforts to help students to think deeply and creatively, what are some of the obstacles you've encountered from students?

ED: I rarely encounter obstacles from children, but that's partly because I don't teach classes of children. I work with two or three children at a time, so I can do what I need to keep them interested. The classes I teach are adults, where the question still comes up because when you teach people in whole classes, when you aren't tending to individuals and their own personal quirks, they start to say, "I don't want to do this, just tell me."

SH: They want you to just hand it to them?

ED: Yes, but the thing is, you can't. If you could, you would, but you can't. You can say whatever words you want but it doesn't connect with anybody and certainly the passion for the subject matter doesn't get conveyed if you're just giving them your words. So I have to work hard to make the subject matter itself be the intriguing focus that gets the students interested.

SH: Do you remember the moment you knew you wanted to be a teacher, and what brought you to that realization?

ED: I was a school teacher for only one year. I started as a teacher educator before I knew anything about being a school teacher so I thought I needed some experience. I still wanted to be a teacher-educator, but I thought I needed to know what it was like to be a school teacher. That was why I became a school teacher. And the reason I wanted to be a teacher-educator was that I recognized what was lacking in my own education and I realized how exciting learning could be when your own ideas are the ones that are being valued and your own excitement is what counts. I wanted all teachers and students to experience that.

SH: Almost everyone who teaches faces a hard time in his or her career. Can you tell us one that was particularly difficult for you?

ED: Well, the one year I was a school teacher was very, very hard and it was the only year I spent as a school teacher because it was so hard.

SH: Why was it so hard?

ED: Well, I was a first-year teacher. That's a sufficient answer for one thing. The second was that I was doing it in French in Quebec, Canada. I know French pretty well, but for one thing, I spoke Parisian French; and for another thing, a teacher needs to have a very subtle repertoire for responding to kids. I didn't have that subtle repertoire for Quebec. Another reason was that I didn't keep the physical materials that I needed in the classroom well organized. I didn't find a way—I don't know why I didn't find a way—to engage the kids in helping me keep the materials organized. So the room became a little physically chaotic.

SH: That's interesting. Do you still have that problem?

ED (laughs): Yeah.

SH: What do you do about it?

ED (laughs): Well, I don't teach school full-time. I think teaching kids is one of the jobs that demands organization more than almost anything else I can think of.

SH: I was going to ask how you worked your way through that but I guess you answered that by saying you didn't go back to it.

ED: Yes, and I feel bad about it, but that's what happened.

SH: Is that a regret in your life?

ED: Yes, I think it would have been good for me to learn how to be a classroom teacher, and I would have loved to have that continuous connection with kids, but I never did.

SH: Does that cause you difficulty in your teaching today?

ED: Somewhat, but not a whole lot, because I'm very open about the fact that I don't know how to make a classroom work—I haven't done that work myself. So teachers appreciate what I do as a teacher of adults, which I've worked at a lot. Also I work with kids in small groups up to five, and teachers appreciate the way I work with kids, even though I haven't figured out how to do it with 30 kids at a time. But I think it would have strengthened my work with teachers if I had figured out how to do that myself.

SH: In what ways have you changed your practice over the years, and what are some of the things that led to those changes?

ED: Well, I haven't changed very much. The other thing that contributed to the way I teach was my work with [Jean] Piaget and [Barbel] Inhelder in which I learned how to be a clinical interviewer, to find out what ideas kids had about things. Piaget and Inhelder were researchers, so I was learning to be a researcher with them. To do that you have to not convey to the kids what *you* want them to think, because then you wouldn't learn anything about what *they* think. So I got very good at getting kids interested in telling me their thoughts and not letting them know when they were pleasing me, and not indicating that this or that was the thought I wanted them to tell me or this was the thought I didn't want them to tell me. I got very good at being neutral and pushing further and learning more and more about their thoughts. Then I realized that listening to people's thoughts was a way to get them interested. I carried that over into my teaching, because I found that when you do that, people get fascinated by subject matters they weren't ever interested in before. If you give them something interesting to think about and are respectful about their ideas about it, they want to keep thinking about things like that. I found that was not just a research approach but also a teaching approach.

As a teacher, I still listen with an acceptance of what people say, and with interest. I continue to ask questions about it and that pushes their own thinking deeply and they can see for themselves if they have contradictions. That came from my research training and that's been the basis of my teaching ever since. I haven't changed that basic view. I've come to be able to explain to myself what I'm doing, better than I did, but I haven't changed what I do.

SH: You've been in teaching for a long time. What is it in what you do and how you think about it that inspires you to continue working?

ED: I love seeing how minds grow. I love seeing how people's thoughts evolve, how they start thinking something, then they realize that doesn't work, and then they find some other way to think about it. I just love seeing the way someone bumps against something they think they can't understand, how they find a way by virtue of looking at it from other angles and find a way to get into it.

SH: You said that the thing that has given you the most satisfaction has been teaching teachers. What do you experience in teaching teachers that is so satisfying?

ED: Teachers already have this great understanding of teaching and learning and it's wonderful to see that understanding shift and deepen. Teaching is such a fascinating topic in itself to have ideas about and teachers are great people to enter into a dialogue with about the topic of teaching.

SH: Do you have advice to give teachers who are in situations where there is lack of support for the learner-centered, active classrooms they're trying to create?

ED: I think an important thing is to find at least one person from whom you do feel support, with whom you can talk about the things that are important to you. I think finding one person, one colleague either in your own school or in a school not too far away or on e-mail to have as your own support—I think that's very critical.

What could I say to teachers having frustrations? It isn't exactly an answer to that question but let me say that those students who have worked with me and are in difficult situations in schools say that the one thing that stands out for them from their work with me is to pay attention to the sense their students are making of whatever they are doing. If you don't understand them, keep probing until you see the sense. Assuming kids have their own ways of making sense and trying to get at [them]—that is what is at the core. That's what teachers have found they can hold onto and can find ways to work with.

SH: Are there things you've seen that give you hope about the ways teachers are doing their work with learners?

ED: Teachers are in a position to let kids realize the power of their minds. This is too important to let go, no matter how great the pressures are to prepare for narrow testing. And I have seen indications that having confidence in their own minds is a significant factor even in doing well on tests—being able to bring the mind to bear on questions they have not seen before—realizing that, if the tests seem to come from left field, it is the tests which are below standard, not they.

SH: Of all you have done, what has given you the greatest sense of satisfaction?

ED: Teaching teachers is certainly what's given me the most satisfaction.

SH: Did you have a mentor?

ED: Not exactly a mentor. Certainly people like Piaget and his co-researcher Inhelder were intellectual giants to me, and I worked with them personally and they cared about my work. Then at the Elementary Science Studies where I got going in education, there was David Hawkins; also my colleague, Mike Savage.

SH: Have you served as a mentor in a formal way?

ED: The closest formal arrangement would be with some of my doctoral students, but no, nothing formal. The book *"Tell Me More": Listening to Learners Explain*, which was published this year, came out of such a collaboration. It's written with six students who are engaged in the same work in which I am engaged. Each one wrote a chapter, each focusing on a different subject matter and different age group of learners. I'm very proud of that book.

SH: Is there something you would like to say to our teacher readers about the work of teaching?

ED: I think being a teacher in a school is about the most complex work there is—the most physically and emotionally demanding work that there is. Because a mind is about as complicated a thing as there is to try to understand, the mind let alone the whole person, and that's what teachers have to do in order to respond to their students. And they have to do it with many, many students at once.

SH: Do you have anything else you would like to tell our teacher readers about teaching?

ED: I have found that when I give people of any age—I do work with kids, but in small numbers, [and] I mainly work with teachers—so, for kids *and* adults, when you give them something substantial to think about, and give them some way to get into it by asking some opening question which provides many, many different ways to respond, and then take people's responses seriously and let them know that their responses will be taken seriously, people really respond. Having their ideas taken seriously is an enormous gift. They put their minds to work in ways they haven't put them to work before and find they can do things, be interested in topics, and have ideas in areas they never thought of before, and they never thought they would ever pay attention to or be able to do before. I have found that when a teacher gets people engaged and gives respectful attention to everybody's thoughts—which includes not just accepting everything at face value but also pushing them, taking an idea seriously in the sense of pushing that idea to see where it goes and whether it does apply in this situation—people really appreciate using their minds that way. And people love it at whatever age.

Another thing is that you can't separate intellect and feelings in the work of the mind. They're both there all the time. Real learning—attentive real learning, deep learning—is playful and frustrating and joyful and discouraging and exciting and sociable and private all at the same time, which is what makes it great.

Chapter Three

YETTA GOODMAN

Learning from the Past, Living in the Present

Yetta Goodman is a major spokes-
person for whole language. She consults with education departments and
speaks at conferences throughout the
United States and in many other nations regarding issues of language,
teaching, and learning with implications for language arts curricula. In
addition to her research in early literacy, miscue analysis, and exploring
reading and writing processes, she has
popularized the term "kid-watching,"
encouraging teachers to be profes-

sional observers of the language and learning development of their students. In her extensive writing, she shows a marked concern for educational
issues and research with a focus on classrooms, students, and teachers.

Goodman is Regents Professor of Education at the University of Ari-
zona, College of Education, in the Department of Language, Reading and
Culture.

Her writings in some 200 publications have influenced educational
thought for the past 20 years. Among those publications is *The Little Over-
coat* (1997).

Interview—Fall 1999

SH: Can you tell us about a learning experience you had as a teacher?
YG: The one experience that comes to mind in terms of how it impacts

my teaching today involves a realization about my teaching. From the very beginning, kids responded well to me as a teacher so I always thought I was a terrific teacher. When I did my student teaching, my supervising teacher thought the kids were responding so well to me that she brought other people to watch me, and I had the same kind of response from principals who thought I could hold onto the group of junior high kids I was working with. Then at some point it dawned on me that I was a performer and not a teacher. I began to see that the students were not involved in their own learning, that, instead, they were responding to me; and that was a very important moment for me in terms of my teaching.

SH: What are some of the ways this influenced what you did with kids?

YG: I began to watch and understand kids. I slowly realized that even though they were responding well to me, there were kids who were not gaining a lot from the experience. I then began to see that I needed to showcase the kids, not have them thinking I was the center of attention. I began to realize the importance of teachers learning how to support kids rather than just constantly leading them.

I realized I had to know my kids better, so I started to learn more about them. I began to sit with them and read with them, so I would know how they responded to what they read. I became much more attentive to them; and I began to understand what strengths they had, to understand how I could help them grow rather than thinking that simply being enthusiastic and charismatic was going to motivate them. I had to learn how to help them to become more aware of their own learning experiences; to be more in control of their learning rather than following my lead; to learn for themselves, not for me. That was a very important thing for me because even though I was very successful with most kids before that, it was not until this happened that I believe I became a real teacher.

SH: What are some of the ways you see that experience in your work today?

YG: From that experience, I began thinking of and using the term "kid-watching" to indicate that we have to know how to observe kids in all kinds of situations. I began to address several questions: How do we discover who kids are? How do we know what they know? How do we build on their knowledge base? I like to observe kids and watch how they read and watch how they write and understand what they do when they are reading and writing and engage them in conversation about their reading and writing. That's important; but I realized it's also important to know how kids are learning out on the playground or how they learn in their homes and their communities. That is something I stress with preservice teachers in my classes today.

SH: How does a teacher learn that?

YG: The best way is to be with kids and be aware. You also have to have some knowledge about what you're going to observe. You need to know how writing develops and how talk develops. You need to know that we talk differently in different contexts. So if we see a kid who is rather silent in the classroom, it's not enough to say this kid is always silent; we have to spend time out on the playground or in the lunchroom watching that kid interact with other kids and observing when and how that kid uses language. I encourage teachers to have lunch with the kids in their classroom, perhaps two or three kids a day, or a couple of times a week. The point is to see kids in different contexts and begin to realize they have lives that are complex and not just the life that's in the classroom.

SH: Can you remember a learning experience you had as a student that stands out in your mind?

YG: There was one experience that happened to me early in my life as a student that had a very strong impact on me. I was a bilingual kid from a poor family in an urban area, and the teachers made me feel I couldn't write or read well. I remember coming home with a report card in second grade with Ds in art and poor grades in handwriting. My mother, who was not an English speaker and was always intimidated about going to school, asked me what the problem was, and I didn't know. So it was a big thing when she decided to go to the school and find out why I was getting such grades. We went to school—I had to translate for her—and we asked the teacher why I got Ds in art. The teacher told my mother I got Ds because I tried so hard. It was a "reward"! Of course, it wasn't to me. All I knew was that it was a grade that was degrading to me, and my mother thought it was terrible. That experience has remained with me all my life.

SH: What influence did that have on your teaching?

YG: It helped me question the whole grading system in our schools. I think grades are very degrading. Even now as a professor I'm facing issues about grading because we have administrators who are concerned that we're giving too many As and Bs. This is in graduate school, where competent students come to us with high grade-point averages, and still there are people who feel you are supposed to have low grades for these fine people.

SH: How do you deal with that?

YG: First of all, I try to help people understand that if I, as a teacher, give low grades, I'm failing as a teacher, because I believe that it's my responsibility to help students in my classes be successful. And even with graduate students, I ask them to hand in their projects and papers ahead of time, to sit down with me so I can help them edit their work or help them think about organizing their work in ways that would be more conducive to the kinds of things we expect of graduate students. I talk a lot about the role of grading with teachers.

SH: It seems everyone who has taught faces a number of hard times or struggles in their careers. Can you think of one that was particularly important to you?

YG: Yes, it's one I'll never forget. The time when I was teaching in California was at the end of the progressive era but it was also during the McCarthy period. We had some big issues to deal with at that time because there was concern that we shouldn't be teaching about the United Nations, for example; and there were problems about teaching about the Soviet Union. It was the whole thing about the Red Menace and the evil aspects of communism. I was teaching seventh and eighth graders at that time, and I always felt it was important to help them become readers of newspapers. To be critical of what was going on in the newspaper was an important part of that process. We had current events every day; kids brought in articles, and there were controversial issues that came up. I remember a young man who said in class, "My father says communism isn't so bad. What do you think about that?" I stood there, and I really didn't know what to say, because I knew it could be a very terrible thing for me if anyone reported that I responded to him in a positive way. So I said, "You know, that's comparative political structures. You're probably going to learn more about that in high school." In other words, I squirmed out of it. It's one of those things you remember all of your life.

After that, it forced me to think about the importance of being strong and brave during controversial times. I think I would handle that differently now because of the thinking I did as a result of that experience. I believe that if we're going to have a democracy, we have to learn how to respond to such controversial issues. Sometimes it means we teachers have to put our own necks on the line if we are going to protect our democracy and protect the rights of kids to say things in class that might be offensive to other people. That experience also helped me understand teachers who are vulnerable and who are not quite sure how to respond when their districts or schools become more authoritarian and begin to mandate all kinds of curricula. Because of that experience, I understand the tensions and know it's very important in a democratic society to deal with and talk about and find multiple ways of responding to those kinds of issues.

SH: Do you see results of that struggle with conscience in your work today?

YG: Oh, of course. I think we have to learn to handle multiple points of view. For example, I have to learn to be able to state my point of view; but, at the same time, if I have a teacher who is, say, a strong phonics advocate in my classes, I strive to find ways of encouraging that person to bring out her point of view, to express it, but also to find evidence to support her point of view. At the same time, I need to be able to express what I believe, too. Then we can have good discussions and explore where these controversies come from and where they play out on our kids.

This is especially important, as we've seen in recent years a move toward an attempt to control teachers, the curriculum, and classrooms. I think some of the issues—like phonics versus whole language, the bilingual issues, the evolutionary versus creationism issues—I think all of these are attempts to control what goes on in classrooms, and to me the important thing is how we help teachers realize they are professionals and have rights as professionals to state their points of view, to explore their belief systems, and to help kids do the same thing.

SH: You are still apparently filled with passion for the work you do and believe you can make a difference. What is it in what you do and how you think about your work that keeps the passion alive for you?

YG: Every year I tell each group of beginning preservice teachers that I work with, "I welcome you to the greatest profession in the world." I believe that. I really think teachers have such an important role to play with young people. They help impact the future leaders, scholars, and workers of our society. So I do have that passion. I think the thing that keeps me going is what I see when I walk into a teacher's classroom and see dynamic learning going on. I see kids involved in solving their own problems and great projects happening. I recall a school in Tucson where two teachers worked together to provide an opportunity for students to explore the concept of lighthouses by opening up their two classrooms so the kids could build their own lighthouses. I know another teacher who organizes her classroom so that half of it is a studio where the kids can write, do artwork, and learn about artists and musicians. It's those kinds of classrooms and the teachers who facilitate them that inspire me.

SH: Are there any other thoughts you would like to convey to teachers?

YG: I would like to emphasize that we need to believe that every kid is a learner and our role is to discover what is exciting to a kid so we can build on that to motivate that kid. I think teachers also need to think of themselves as learners in their own classrooms, to be aware of how our kids are responding to the classroom situation all the time. We've got to think of teaching as a composition. Every time you're in a classroom with kids, you are composing or orchestrating a new classroom. Everyone's involved in that orchestration or composition; and, working together, growth of learning takes place as people interact with and encourage each other to create an exciting learning experience.

Chapter Four

GRANT WIGGINS

The Evolution of a Teacher Educator

Grant Wiggins is the president of Grant Wiggins and Associates in Monmouth Junction, New Jersey. He consults with schools, districts, and state education departments on a variety of reform matters; organizes national conferences and workshops; and develops video, software, and print materials on assessment and curricular change. Wiggins has consulted with some of the most influential assessment-reform initiatives in the country (including Kentucky's performance-based system and Vermont's portfolio system); established two statewide consortia devoted to assessment reform; and designed a performance-based and teacher-run portfolio assessment prototype for the state of North Carolina.

He earned an Ed.D. from Harvard University and a B.A. from St. John's College in Annapolis, Maryland.

Wiggins is the author of *Educative Assessment* and *Assessing Student Performance*. He and Jay McTighe are co-authors of *Understanding by Design*.

Wiggins's many articles have appeared in such journals as *Educational Leadership* and *Phi Delta Kappan*. His work is grounded in 14 years of secondary school teaching and baseball coaching.

Wiggins has fronted four rock 'n' roll bands as a singer and guitar player. He coaches the Little League teams of both his sons. His favorite job as coach is hitting fungoes (to hit fungoes means to hit grounders and fly balls to players in practice—especially fly balls—with a special long and thin fungo bat for extra oomph) and pitching at batting practice. He does all the family cooking.

Wiggins can be reached at grant@grantwiggins.org.

Interview—Summer 1999

SH: At Foxfire, we believe reflecting on memorable learning experiences can inform our own teaching practice. Can you tell us about one of your memorable learning experiences?

GW: One that stands out is actually negative and positive at the same time. It was in graduate school. I was at Harvard in the School of Education in my first year and was taking some courses in liberal arts—a philosophy course. I was in over my head in this course on Emmanuel Kant taught by a visiting English don from Oxford who was very snooty, and it was one of those self-doubting times when I was prepared not only to quit the course but to quit graduate school. The reading was very hard and I felt it was not going to work. I projected my experience from this one class to all my classes and thought, "Well, if this is what it's going to be like, maybe I'm not cut out for it."

I was in the discussion section of the course for graduate students. All the other grad students were philosophy Ph.D.s and much more knowledgeable than I was. In fact, all of them were able to read Kant in German. It was a daunting experience for me. I was sitting there only half paying attention and just brooding and feeling miserable; and serendipitously the professor said, "Well, we all remember what Wiggins said the other day." I kind of looked up . . . I was stunned. I didn't even know what he was referring to. I must have had a funny look on my face because he repeated it. I hadn't realized he had *ever* noticed anything I'd said and had been feeling pretty much like a cipher in this discussion.

It was just one of those serendipitous things—I might well have dropped out had he not said that at that particular moment. So it was a wonderful lesson to me that students are very dependent on how they feel about themselves as students—that they have to be noticed and rewarded for what they do or they can't succeed. Feedback is vital, in other words.

In thinking of other learning experiences, I would say that much of who I am has been shaped not so much by a singular learning experience but by my experiences as an undergraduate at St. John's College, the Great Books school. There, seminars are primarily student-run, with the exception of probing questions and redirections by the tutors. Four years of that gives you a fundamentally different view of what education is and ought to be, so it was a very formative experience that affected my approach to teaching when I was a teacher and now in working with adults to inform education. I take that with me wherever I go.

SH: Can you tell us some of the ways this experience influenced what you did with kids?

GW: When I began to teach, I was quite deliberate to replicate that St. John's experience. I trained students to be not only discussion participants but to be discussion leaders. I told them my job was to make myself only the facilitator. However, over time I realized I had to *coach* them in how to be participants. That, coaching students, was missing at St. John's. I said, "Let's treat this like a sport. There are different roles to play in this discussion." And I gave them roles, such as the person with the compass whose job was to say, "I think we're lost here; we need to get back on track." Another role was the person whose job was to pay attention to people who looked like they had something to say but were being ignored by the group. I made the roles very explicit, gave them cute names, and we would take turns sort of trying them on. So for 10 minutes at a time, they played one of these roles. In the last 2 weeks of the course, my only role was to observe and give feedback as if they were playing a game.

SH: What are some ways you see your learning experience as a graduate student in your work today?

GW: Today I spend all my time working with adults in courses they take for professional development, but I think there are ways in which all the stories come together. Adults also need to feel they are competent and their work is valuable and that somebody notices them. I always have to keep in mind the Kant story because some of what I think I do and demand of adults is pretty difficult, and so I always have to remind myself to help them feel successful. Second, part of what makes so much of professional development challenging is that there is such a built-up tradition of fatalism or cynicism or, at best, a sort of skepticism about whether these experiences will be valuable. I think I can make it a valuable experience because I have learned the St. John's lesson—to make it thought-provoking and to engage them in intellectual work that matters through the Socratic seminar approach and by applying what I've gained through my own background in teaching, philosophy, and writing curriculum.

SH: Do you remember the moment you knew you wanted to be a teacher?

GW: Actually, I do remember the very moment. I was a high school tenth-grade student at a boarding school in Connecticut. We had Saturday classes in those days, and I had a wise teacher for Algebra II who had to go away for the weekend and asked me to teach the class. He said to me, "I want you to teach the Saturday class instead of my just assigning some work to everybody." I think he sensed I was enough of a good student and enough of a screw up that this responsibility would be a good thing for me. He was right. I prepared very hard for it, and I was surprised at how difficult it was. I had no idea that what I understood, would be hard for other people to understand, and that puzzle has stayed with me to this day. I think I'm more aware than perhaps a lot of teachers just how *un*obvious what we want to teach really is to a student who doesn't get it. I knew I wanted to tackle that problem and I also knew I liked the life of teaching, coaching, and working with kids.

SH: It seems everyone who teaches faces times of struggle. Can you think of one that was particularly important to you?

GW: What comes to mind for me is the doubts that one has about one's abilities or whether this is really the profession for them. Where I have had real doubts is in working with adults. I think teaching adults is extraordinarily difficult. They're more set in their ways than young children, more inflexible, and more demanding. Yet one of the really valuable lessons I have learned in working with adults is that they are quite free in giving you blunt feedback. That has had a profound impact on me both negatively and positively. Practically no teacher understands until they've worked with adults that there is a constant gap between what you intended and what you in effect accomplished. But because there is all this constant feedback [with adult students], you learn more about teaching. We rarely get this kind of feedback from younger students. Some adult students think you have nothing to offer and that you're a terrible teacher and they tell you so. It was brutal at first. But I came out the other side thinking, "I'm a much better teacher because I got that feedback." It was kind of a crucible. It really stung me internally. I'm pretty good at masking that; but, internally, I brooded for days and days and wondered if I could ever be good enough to get beyond some of that negative feedback. Once that feeling died down, I got to work improving the presentation and the materials, and the feedback got better.

SH: When teaching young kids, was there a moment during that time that changed the way you interacted with students and affected your teaching from then on?

GW: There are two things that stand out. One comes from my early interest in feedback and thinking of teaching as similar to coaching a sport and therefore [saying,] "let's rerun the action." I asked the AV guy (in those days there were no VCRs) to bring the huge, cumbersome reel-to-reel videotape recorder and camera to my class to tape one of the seminars so I could not only think about my own role as seminar facilitator but see how students appeared on camera. It gave me an opportunity to just observe it. I was horrified to discover some of my mannerisms and language usage. The one that stood out was that I must have used the word "obvious" three times in a span of 5 minutes. "Obvious" is precisely what it *isn't* to the students, so I was determined from that point on to pay very close attention to what it felt like to be in their place and what language or mannerisms would make them more comfortable.

The other experience had to do with a particular student who was an advisee of mine and an athlete on my soccer team and lived in the dorm with me and was in my class all in the same term. In class he was absolutely disengaged, always distracted, always looking sleepy eyed. In all the other venues, he was alert, confident, productive, and pleasant to be around. It was a reminder the teacher often gets in a boarding school environment, in which you get to see kids in various contexts and realize that underneath that "slug" passing notes in the back row is a really interesting, mature, and productive kid in many other ways. That had a profound effect on me. I never saw either the student or the adult as one-dimensional again. I'm always wondering what makes them tick as a person. I know that there is often an interesting person behind dull eyes and that my challenge is to put a spark in those eyes.

SH: Are there any lessons or thoughts you'd like to convey to our teacher readers?

GW: Well, I think there are a couple of lessons. I wouldn't generalize from my own quirky experience too much but there are a couple of common threads. One is that, as Piaget knew and now others know, it's important that everyone come to see that the student doesn't understand as much as you think the student understands. Whether we look at Piaget's work or at the most recent literature in student misconception/student misunderstanding, there's a Pandora's box that opens for the naive teacher. Maybe that metaphor is not right because although it does unleash chaos in your teaching world, it's a good chaos. There's a door that opens into this extraordinary, strange, sobering, interesting, intriguing, thought-provoking world of, "Gee, how is it possible that the kids didn't get that? I thought they did; I thought they should have; I was so clear." We can do better in curriculum and assessment to reveal this to people. As soon as we reveal this, because teachers are well motivated, they'll deal with it. They won't turn their backs on the lesson—one that can be summarized in a little quip I always use with teachers in workshops: "You should really think of the student as innocent of understanding until proven guilty by a preponderance of evidence." And a corollary to that is (though it's true more of the older student, it's not a bad maxim to work under with students of all ages): "Assume that the student is trying to please you without really understanding, since that's the easiest course for the student." The flip side of that is *that's* when teaching becomes interesting and not just routine. It may be initially depressing, but *then* teaching becomes an enormously interesting and invigorating challenge. I've seen that firsthand with many of the teachers I've worked with. There's a thought experiment we always do when we teach people to design units: "What is a predictable misunderstanding a student will have about this subject? If you can predict it, what are you doing to counteract it?" Just that simple thought experiment causes us as teachers to see things in a new light and to become intrigued by what there is for us to learn there.

TEACHING AND
THE POWER OF STORY

The interviews in Part II reveal the power of story—whether those of students or of teachers—to influence the thinking and the personal and professional lives of both.

Chapter Five

ROBERT COLES

Taking Learning to Heart

Robert Coles is a child psychiatrist, physician, teacher, writer, and editor who has spent his working life trying to understand the lives of children. The result of that effort has been a series of books that tell of the particular lives of boys and girls who live in different regions of the United States and in foreign countries.

A research psychiatrist for Harvard University Health Services and a professor of Psychiatry and Medical Humanities at Harvard Medical School, Coles has taught courses at Harvard's Medical School, Law School, School of Education, and Extension School. He is also the editor of *DoubleTake Magazine*, a community service-based magazine dedicated to preserving the American documentary tradition through essays, photography, poetry, and fiction.

Since 1961, Coles has published more than 1,500 articles, reviews, and essays in newspapers, magazines, journals, and anthologies. His 60-plus books include: *Children of Crisis* (in five volumes), *Women of Crisis* (with Jane Coles, in two volumes), *The Moral Life of Children*, *The Political Life of Children*, *The Call of Stories: Teaching and the Moral Imagination*, *Lives of Moral Leadership*, *The Spiritual Life of Children*, *The Eyes Meeting the World: The Youngest Parents*, and *The Moral Intelligence of Children*.

Among the many awards Robert Coles has received are the Pulitzer Prize (1973), the Presidential Medal of Freedom (1998), the American Psychiatric Association Distinguished Service Award (2000), and the National Humanities Medal (2002).

Coles lives outside Boston, Massachusetts. Two sons, Robert and Daniel, are physicians. A third son, Michael, went to medical school and is now a documentary photographer and writer. Coles has three grandchildren.

Interview—Winter 2000

SH: Can you tell us about a memorable learning experience you had as a student?

RC: The one that comes to my mind is a fifth-grade experience with a teacher named Bernecia Avery. She was a very strong-minded and vigorous teacher, and I vividly remember the American history she taught us, and I vividly remember her teaching us about American history and the tragedy of the Civil War. I remember her telling us about Abraham Lincoln. And then I remember seeing her crying, as did others in the class. We all sat there fixed and silent, not restless as we sometimes were when she spoke. She was in tears telling us about Lincoln and telling us about his decency, the way he felt for others, even as he was trying to advance himself. She made that distinction so clearly to us—that the important thing in life was not only to do well but to think of others. She held him up as an example. She then told us about the people Lincoln had wanted to help. Not only the people we now call African-Americans, but also the ordinary poor and impoverished people of the country. She told us how Lincoln deeply regretted the Civil War—the fact that a terrible war had taken place. In other words, she turned the Civil War into a melancholy look at history— insisted that we ought to think about history not only in the abstract but in the concrete. She urged us to think of Lincoln's example so that we might become more and more like him in our own lives. I remember her saying "in your own lives," and I vividly recall her telling us that the important thing was not the dates of the Civil War, or which president Lincoln was numerically in the history of America, or where he was born or died. The important thing was what kind of *person* he was, what kind of *character* he had, and how we might learn from him. In fact, she said, "You can learn from Lincoln." I still remember those words. Now this was in its own way a break with the usual forms of education we were experiencing, not only in her classroom but in other classrooms. And I began to realize at that age, as I came home to talk to my parents about it and my friends about it, that a teacher had given us a dramatic, personal, moral moment. She had told us not only about someone, a president, but also about something and someone who *mattered* to her; and she had brought history alive and connected it to personal introspection and storytelling in a very urgent and compelling manner. The result was that I remember that moment to this day, and it was well over a half a century ago. In that moment my own working life began, because I always think of her. I remember a teacher who could break not only with the past in general, but with her own past as a teacher. She could give us a surprising kind of instruction that clung to us heart, mind, and soul. So there's a memory for you—what a memory! For me, it shows how memory can connect to storytelling and to moral reflection in the listener's mind, as well as in the storyteller's mind.

SH: What are some of the ways you see this experience influencing what you do with students?

RC: I try to teach in such a way that the books we read also become books we hold close to ourselves, to our lives. I try to emphasize the way fiction can get connected to our lives, and I emphasize the capacity of our eyes and our ears in our lives to prompt in us moral reflection. In my course, "The Literature of Social Reflection," there's a kind of moral reflection that goes on. By the time we've gone through Zora Neal Hurston's novel, *Their Eyes Were Watching God*, or the works of Flannery O'Connor or Walker Percy, we are not only reading novels, but remembering in our own lives our ongoing stories, with various chapters and books to them. We become self-conscious in a reflective way that prompts us to think about the puzzles of life, the accidents and incidents that shape us, but also the moral urgencies that come toward us and demand our response.

SH: You have many roles in life, including writer, editor, child psychiatrist, and professor. Yet I wonder if you don't see yourself primarily as a teacher.

RC: I do. I regard myself as a parent and grandparent who has taught children. There's a lot of teaching to be done within a family, and a lot of learning to do—the learning one experiences courtesy of one's children and grandchildren and of one's wife or husband. Also, I teach the course I've mentioned, and I work as a volunteer in an elementary school and a high school in Boston, which I do simply because I feel invigorated by contact with children and, inevitably, I learn from them. So I do love teaching. And I am a physician. I started out in pediatrics. When you're a pediatrician and a child psychiatrist, you effectively learn to take care of children and to teach them the best way you can by offering them thoughts and by interpreting things that you've learned in a way that makes sense to them. I also work very hard with the visual side of childhood. I'm always sitting with children and they're drawing pictures and I'm drawing pictures, and this is an endless source of pleasure for me because I learn so much from looking at what children choose to draw and the way they portray themselves or their friends and the world around them or their parents or teachers. It's a privilege to do this kind of work. Even then I'm a bit of a teacher, because the children sometimes want help or "guidance" as they try to represent visually on paper thoughts that they have. I work with them as best I can to enable them to "see" what they are showing me—to understand themselves.

SH: You've said that your magazine, *DoubleTake*, is a new classroom for you. Can you say more about how you see the magazine as a classroom and what you hope to accomplish through it?

RC: I first came on the idea for such a magazine while doing a profile for *The New Yorker* on Eugene Smith, the photographer. One day I was asking him questions and he had *Life* magazine near him. He picked it up and said, "Someday there'll be a magazine that will have what *Life* magazine offers—pictures that connect us to everyday events visually—and will have the kind of writing that *The New Yorker* has." That caused me to stop and think about what such a magazine would be like that would have the wonderful fiction and nonfiction of *The New Yorker* and the visual images of *Life*. That was in the back of my mind as I began to think about *DoubleTake*. I see *DoubleTake* as a venue for the reader to come to terms with life and people through the camera and through listening to words, responding to language.

The magazine has importance for me because I *am* a teacher (of course, all parents, every day, are teachers!). In the class I mentioned earlier, I connect novels and poems and pictures to relatively privileged students who go to Harvard College. And sometimes to augment the short stories, books, and poems we study, I take in photographs, pictures, slides of images by artists. For example, when we studied Tillie Olsen's short story, "I Stand Here Ironing," I showed the students slides of two paintings—one by Degas and one by Picasso of a woman standing ironing. Here were two artists and a writer of fiction who converged in their sensibility, their responsiveness to what it means to stand there, with that iron, and try to straighten out a tie, a shirt, a dress, and, of course, straighten out life, or straighten out one's experiences or obligations in life, helping others by taking care of their clothing, or whatever. We went on and on and on in that manner. "I Stand Here Ironing" is really a story of a mother who, as she goes about her daily chores, thinks about her children, her experiences with others. It's a powerful story and the visual images helped us. And I began to think one day—what if I could carry that kind of learning and teaching into other classrooms? It was at that point that I remembered Eugene Smith talking about a new magazine that he hoped someday would arrive that would offer the best of the visual and the best of the written.

So *DoubleTake* is in a sense an outgrowth of my own teaching life. It's an effort to make that teaching available to others who don't come into my college classroom. I realized we can spread this expanded view of things other ways than by going personally into a particular school or college. We can do it more generally through a magazine. So we regard the magazine as an educational institution.

SH: Do you see a need for teachers to lead their students to make connections between what they are learning and their own lives and the world around them?

RC: Oh, I certainly do. You know teachers obviously have the responsibility to offer certain instruction, but they are also guides—moral and philosophical guides. The eyes of all those children are on them. Their voices are constantly attended by the children—or teachers certainly want that to happen. And with all that opportunity goes a responsibility. We are often at our best when we connect ideas either to our own lives or to the lives of others. So this approach or attitude, on the part of a teacher, can make for an intense, compelling, and memorable classroom experience. One always offers a *caveat* and a concern, in the sense that any good thing can be corrupted. The point is not to become self-indulgent and let one's own personal experiences dominate the classroom requirement that one become a medium for others. One always has a responsibility not only to the students before one, but to the writers, the subject matter to which one is ultimately responsible. If I can't teach Raymond Carver's extraordinary fiction without turning it into an exercise in self-indulgence, I'm in real trouble. But there are moments reading Carver or other writers when one can begin to study those writers in a personally alive manner which one conveys to the class: "You know I was reading these writers just before class, and they got to my heart and soul"; or whatever way one wants to put it, such as, "They really stay with you and I would encourage you as you read these stories to take them to heart." That's what we are trying to get at—to take learning to heart—and one hopes one's students do as well. One is mindful of factuality, of tradition, of convention, of history itself, of chronology, of methods and requirements and standards. All of these are important. Still, a little bit of heartfelt feeling in all of this can go a long way, both for a student and for the teacher.

SH: Everyone who has taught has faced a number of hard times or struggles in their careers. Can you think of one that was particularly important to you?

RC: Well, I taught in a classroom in New Orleans during the early days of integration, and we were working with kids who had to go through mobs in order to get into school. My wife, Jane Hallowell, and I were very discouraged by the mobs outside the school, but also by the failure of the city and state to respond to a historical moment with any degree of moral courage, certainly not the moral courage the children demonstrated. Jane and I began to wonder why it is that with the people we saw, teachers in a cosmopolitan area, a sophisticated city—why that happens. A few years later, the same thing happened in Boston. Boston went through a similar struggle, and the schools there failed as wretchedly as they did in New Orleans. The people who were running the schools were not as steadfast, brave, and courageous as some of the families of the children were who were trying to get through a difficult moment in the city's history by bearing up and pulling together. I began to wonder about schools because I felt that what really mattered in the schools was not the teachers and the school officials but, of course, the children, who supposedly needed the help of the teachers and the schools. So it gives one a great deal of moral pause when there seems to be so little moral stamina on the part of prominent educators and school systems—yet plenty on the part of the young children yet to be "educated." One then begins to wonder what "education" does, and for whom.

SH: How did that feel and how did you work your way through it?

RC: Well, it was very discouraging, but my father reminded me that when Hitler took power in Germany, education and cultural station did not necessarily give people immunity from Nazi hatred. I'll never forget that he put it that way. He reminded me that some of the most prominent figures in Germany—educators, college professors, presidents of universities—quickly fell in line with the Nazis. I had never thought about it that way. I knew about Hitler and what happened in Germany, but I didn't stop to think of what happened to the people in that society, who, by the way, included ministers who endorsed Hitler. I realized after thinking about that conversation with my father that, in the clutch, moral virtue is not necessarily to be equated with educational achievement.

That was tough to learn firsthand in New Orleans and Boston. And maybe that is something one has to offer to one's classes and remind one's students—that, yes, you want to do well in school, on the S.A.T. test, because these things tell us about certain kinds of cognitive development; but they do *not* tell us about moral or emotional development! And *that* is something we need to be "teaching." I hope we want our students to do well academically, yes; but we also want them to develop morally and emotionally.

SH: Looking back at your career, what are the things you have done that give you the greatest sense of accomplishment and satisfaction?

RC: The meetings I've had with children! The privilege of learning something about their lives, learning with them about how their minds and hearts work—what they perceive to matter, what they feel matters—conversations with them, learning from them. In a sense what I try to emphasize in my books is that children (through their stories related, remembered, and conveyed) are in their own way our educators.

SH: Earlier you mentioned drawing with children. How do you use drawing with children and how do you go about it?

RC: To me, it is my way into their minds, into their memories. Through their drawings, they are telling me, they are literally picturing, what occurs to them, what they remember, or what they hold dear, or what they find scary. I've learned to do this with children; and that way I've learned from them. After you've done this for a number of years, you begin to understand how a particular drawing can teach you. And you also have to connect the drawing to the life of the one who does the drawing. What I do is ask the children to tell me about the picture, to talk about the picture they have drawn, to tell me what I should make of it. So I enlist the children as interpreters, as well as artists. That's very important—to ask for the support and advice of the children. I learned this from two of my own teachers, Erik Erikson and Anna Freud. I was extremely lucky to work with both of them as a student. I've written long books about both of them, with a great deal of pleasure—because the one who has written about children is the one who learned to write about children from those two. That was a very important part of my life—to be able to call upon them for their counsel, for their interpretations, for their thoughts, for their advice, for their recommendations. So, my luck has been, on the one hand, to have those two, and on the other, to meet all those school children, my teachers.

SH: You've been in education a long time. What is it in what you do and how you think about your work that inspires you to continue working?

RC: I couldn't do without it! I couldn't do without those wonderful students, or young children, or high schoolers, or college students. I love the opportunity to read yet again books that have meant so much to me, or to look again at photographs or paintings that have meant so much to me and to share that. But also very important is to learn from others as they respond to what I've initiated. Just the other day, I was working with a group of teachers, and there was a wonderful response to Raymond Carver's fiction by a teacher, Steven Ruthford, who comes from Bellingham, Washington. (Carver lived not far from there for a while.) He's a wonderfully thoughtful, sensitive, and knowing person, a westerner who teaches high school children biology and chemistry. He's also an avid and thoughtful reader, and listening to him respond to Raymond Carver's writing was a wonderfully exhilarating education. When I hear someone take Carver to heart in an astute and broad way and make Carver yet again alive for me, as well as the rest of us in that class, I think to myself—this is a great day; and I am so privileged to be able to spend a couple of hours in a seminar and think about Raymond Carver again with the help of this very fine and articulate and reflective member of the class. I felt myself a grateful member of *his* class.

SH: Is there anything else you would like to say to teachers about teaching?

RC: All of us who teach need to remember that we have a wonderful gift granted us, which is to encounter the young and be part of their lives. I would also bring up the wonderful way Walker Percy expressed it when he talked about the responsibility we all have before we die to "hand one another along" through life. By that he means hand one another along personally, intellectually, and morally. It's a great job, a very special job to have that privilege to connect with young people of another generation, to connect with the future and to try to help that future become broader, richer, and stronger. In a sense, our students become our comrades-in-teaching! Teaching often can be a mutuality, a joint endeavor!

Chapter Six

DONALD GRAVES

Articulating Learning Experiences That Work

Donald Graves's teaching and re-searching background is based solidly in hands-on experience. He has been a teacher; school principal; language supervisor; education director; and director of language in bilingual, English as a Second Language, and special programs. Moving to the university teaching level, he has been co-director of an undergraduate urban teacher preparation program and professor in an early childhood program. He was Professor of Education at the University of New Hampshire for 19 years, where he also directed the Writing Process Laboratory. This extensive experience gives him a keen sense of the real concerns, pressures, and issues of both the classroom teacher and the researcher. His book, *Writing Teachers and Children at Work*, has become a best-seller throughout the English-speaking world and has revolutionized the way writing is taught in schools.

In addition to his writing, Graves travels regularly throughout the United States presenting keynote addresses, seminars, workshops, and inservice training sessions.

Among Graves's numerous books are: *The Energy to Teach* (2000), *How to Catch a Shark and Other Stories* (1998), *A Fresh Look at Writing* (1996), and *Build a Literate Classroom* (1991).

Graves lives in Jackson, New Hampshire. He is an avid bicyclist and recently returned from a biking tour in Europe.

Interview—Spring 2000

SH: Do you remember the moment you knew you wanted to be a teacher, and what brought you to that realization?

DG: Well, this may sound strange, but my father was a superintendent of schools, and for the longest time I said, "No way am I going to teach." Then—I don't know whether he did this surreptitiously or not, but—he said, "Why don't you come down and observe some first-grade teachers?" So I did. I was quite taken with the very good teaching that was going on. I thought about it: I was just getting out of the service—I was in the Coast Guard for 4 years—and I was married with one child and another on the way, and I needed to eat. I decided then that I would teach. So I took an 8-week teacher intensive training course to learn how to teach. Can you imagine that—an 8-week course? They were desperate in those days. The pay was so low that they were hunting for anyone who was even willing to take any kind of training to teach, so after 8 weeks I ended up teaching 39 seventh graders.

SH: I imagine it was quite an experience for you walking in for the first day.

DG: Oh, yes, but I was so ignorant I had no idea what I was taking on.

SH: Can you tell us about a memorable learning experience you had as a student that had an impact on your teaching? [Editor's Note: For more of Donald Graves's memorable learning experiences, read *How to Catch a Shark and Other Stories*, his collection of 18 such stories.]

DG: When I was a high school student in Spanish, we had a professor who wanted us to sing in Spanish, and we thought he was crazy—we could hardly make our way in this class—we were in total immersion Spanish, which meant we spoke no English. But he was a very fine piano player, and he sat down and started to play these songs. At first, maybe two or three joined in. As boys, we were very nervous about letting our voices go—they were changing and all that. But after a couple of catchy songs, we realized we were starting to pick up the language in ways we hadn't before. After that day it got so that we begged him to play the piano and sing on Fridays. "Well," he said, "I'll do it once a week provided you work your tails off Monday through Thursday." It's amazing how much of a language you can learn through songs; I still have those songs with me today.

The thing I learned most about that was the importance of being immersed in a subject, having fun with it. It was this risk-taking on the teacher's part—totally being himself and enjoying the music that was an invitation in its own right. I enjoyed language anyway, but that way in was one I've used in my teaching all these years—you don't go in part way;

you go in all the way. You have to do it yourself—he sang with us. He wasn't asking us to do anything that he didn't do himself. That has been very important to me. Immersion. Do it with your students. Invite them in to do something that you're already doing yourself.

SH: Do you remember a significant learning experience you had as a teacher?

DG: OK. I was sort of a teacher-researcher at this point, and I was doing research on writing and was talking to a boy [Michael] in second grade. He had drawn a very nice picture and was starting to write down below. Michael said to me, "You know, Mr. Graves, you like the writing but I like the drawing." The impact that had on me was I realized that as teachers we're often doing things for our own ends when the kid is seeing something much more significant. So I said to him, "Well, tell me about it." The amount of language he produced from the drawing was ten times what he did in his writing. In that statement, I realized the place drawing had in relation to writing for him. His drawing was his rehearsal for his writing. He worked out his ideas through illustration and then wrote what he wanted to say after doing that. What he was able to write was quite dependent on his drawing.

SH: What did that experience do to you? Did it change the way you interacted with kids?

DG: What it did was to say to me, "Look, you've got your way, but you better listen to the kids." For example, in retrospect, what I learned from it was that most times you look back and say, "Oooh, this is what I should have done." For example, I was director of a reading clinic for 5 years in a city in upstate New York, and we gave kids all kinds of batteries of reading tests to find out what their problems were. But because of my experience with Michael, it hit me—4 years back when I was running the reading clinic, I never asked [Michael] what he thought the problem was with his reading. In other words, we don't take the time to ask kids what their perception is of the very thing we're teaching. So retrospectively, what I learned from Michael was very important.

SH: Do you see those experiences in your work today?

DG: Sure. For example, whenever I go into a room, I'll move around among the kids and deliberately look for something that is working for a kid. Maybe he's put a full stop or period in just the right place—maybe the only one on the page. I'll say, "You know, you got that period just right. How did you know to put it there? I'm really curious because you got it just right." At that point the youngster has to explain how he got it—maybe it's pure luck, and that's all right. What they often say is, "What I was doing at that time . . ." They start to come up with language stories or learning stories and that's what they need; they need learning stories for when things are working. I'm learning too; I'm curious to know all the ways kids decide where a period goes. Maybe the kid has just written, "I caught a fish. It was bigger than me." "What do you mean it was bigger?" I might ask. And the story starts to unfold.

In other words, I'm learning that we simply don't ask kids often enough how things are working. In the past when something wasn't working right, I'd say, "What did you do that for?" Well, if he knew, he wouldn't have done it. But in this case I want them to articulate with learning stories so they can apply it to other places.

SH: It seems everyone who has taught has faced a number of hard times in their careers. Can you think of one that was particularly difficult for you?

DG: Sure. It was when I was a senior in college. We had two papers to write on tragedy and two on comedy. My professor did not want me to write a thesis on the Russian authors but on the English ones. But I was stubborn and chose to write about Prince Andrew Bolknosky in *War and Peace* because I was struggling with conscientious objection. I had a friend, Ted Davey—this would have been in September of 1951. Ted was with me at the beginning of school—the two of us threw the javelin on the track team. He went to his mailbox the first day of college and there was an envelope in there that said, "You are hereby ordered to report to active duty." Ted said, "They can't do that." He got on the phone, came back, and said, "Yeah, they can. I guess this is it for me for school this year." He was immediately shipped to Korea. Eight weeks later, I learned that he was killed by a sniper.

So I was struggling with Ted's death; I was struggling with tragedy in Prince Bolknosky's life; I was struggling with, "Do I really want to go and kill somebody?" I wrote the paper and when I got it back it had a D+ on it and one line written by the professor: "Would you please change your typewriter ribbon." I went crazy. I subsequently flunked three exams I was so upset. I was so absorbed in this struggle of Ted's death and Bolknosky, who is also severely wounded while in combat, not unlike Ted Davey. I got that response and I built a career on it—no way would I ever respond to a student's paper like that.

SH: How did you work your way through that?

DG: I went on academic probation. I finally came out on the other side. Of course, ultimately I did go into the service and that's why I chose the U.S. Coast Guard. But that sting was with me, I would say, for the next 10 years. It wasn't until I really got to the point where I in turn was a teacher of writing at the university that I was finally able to do something about it by helping other students and preparing teachers to never do that. If I talk about it, I'm still a little bit angry. But I at least worked around it so I don't see myself as a complete loser. That's exactly how I felt. I wasn't strong enough to say to myself: "He's wrong." Deep down, I knew he was wrong, but he took the rug out from under me as far as just totally ignoring what I thought was worthwhile in that struggle, and so I was really hurt in terms of thinking I really had something to say about something.

SH: Can you tell me about a hard time you had during your teaching career that you had to work your way through?

DG: It was getting through those first 3 months as a teacher—the time when you're all show and you're trying to put up the big front. Just to show how little I had learned when I first taught, when my students handed in papers, I corrected them. I wasn't going after them as people or their ideas, but I really went after their spelling and punctuation and all. I wanted them to be impressed at how hard I was working to make them good writers in all of this, and it wasn't until—picture this—until the following March that I realized I was correcting the same things in March that I was in September. Of course, the kids are saying, "Hey, he's doing such a good job, let him do it."

I wasn't teaching. Correcting is not teaching. Anyone can correct. Teaching is showing, showing how to punctuate with stuff on the overhead or stuff on the chalkboard.

SH: So how did you change your practice?

DG: I started to show more; I started to correct less. I started to have them keep records on what they were succeeding in, and I would say, "Oh, now you're getting there. Add this to your list of things you know how to do." It took me quite a while before I really learned how to show the kids how to punctuate, how to write dialogue. You can spend the rest of your life learning how to do that well. Good teaching is showing and that's what lasts. That's the big question: How do you teach in a way that it lasts?

SH: You have been in teaching a long time. What is it in what you do and how you think about it that inspires you to continue working?

DG: In writing, there's always a new idea just around the bend. And if you are writing without any preconceived notion of what it ought to be, that's when you get surprises. It's the same with teaching—there's always a kid there who is going to surprise me if I listen well enough, if I observe well enough. And the longer you work at it, it's the surprises, the delights that keep you going. That for me is what it's all about. How can I put my show aside and be honest with the kid and myself? It's hard to be honest both ways.

SH: Did you have any mentors in your career?

DG: Sure, some big ones. Don Murray. When I finished my dissertation, which prepares no one to learn to teach writing, I had a terrible case of dissertationese, and he really helped me to write simply and directly. He was a colleague when I first started teaching at the university.

I truly had no good teachers of writing up to that point, and I was 43 years old. I just lucked out that I happened to be at the same university with the person whom I consider to be the finest teacher of writing I've ever met—before, during, and after. He's an absolute genius at finding out what it is you have to say and helping you to say it. He'll read four pages of your stuff and say, "It begins over here on page four." He'll turn to page six and say, "This second paragraph—this sounds like you—write that way." His advice is so economical; he chooses the one thing that you need to focus on, and that's what good teachers do. If you give a kid 10 things that need to be fixed, you're not a good teacher. It's just the one thing that will make the difference, and you know the field, and you know the student so well that you are able to choose that one thing with precision, and that's what Murray does.

SH: Is there anything about teaching you'd like to relay to teachers?

DG: Be yourself and, if you find people are coming along asking you to do things that are not you, it's going to affect the way you relate to your students. When you write, write with your students. You can't tell someone how to write; you have to show them your own writing. Besides, why should the kids have all the fun? It's for us first and then we'll let them in on the secret—just like Tom Sawyer painted the white fence.

Chapter Seven

VIVIAN G. PALEY

Listening to Children's Stories

Vivian Gussin Paley writes and teaches about the world of young children. She examines their stories and play, their logic, and their thinking, searching for meaning in the social and moral landscapes of classroom life.

A kindergarten teacher for 37 years, Paley brings her storytelling/story-acting and discussion techniques to children, teachers, and parents throughout the world.

Her books include: *A Child's Work: The Importance of Fantasy Play* (2004), *In Mrs. Tully's Room* (2001), *The Kindness of Children* (1999), *Kwanzaa and Me: A Teacher's Story* (1995), *You Can't Say You Can't Play* (1992), *The Boy Who Would Be a Helicopter* (1990), *Bad Guys Don't Have Birthdays* (1988), *Mollie Is Three* (1986), *Boys and Girls* (1984), *Wally's Stories* (1981), and *White Teacher* (1979).

Among awards she has received are: a Lifetime Achievement American Book Award from the Before Columbus Foundation in 1998; the Harvard University Press annual Virginia and Warren Stone Prize for the outstanding book about education and society in 1997 for her book *The Girl with the Brown Crayon* and the NCTE (National Council of Teachers of English) David H. Russell Award for Distinguished Research in the Teaching of English in 1999 for the same book; and the John Dewey Society's Outstanding Achievement Award for the year 2000.

Vivian Paley found that walking in the woods and on the beach in northern Wisconsin was always the best way for her to think about her classroom. She says it is now the best way for her to think about children in other teachers' classrooms.

Interview—Winter 1998

SH: In your 37-year teaching career, what memorable learning experiences stand out to you?

VP: I think of an African-American mother who told me that she wanted her child's differences recognized. This had a big effect on me and was very significant in leading to my first book, *White Teacher.* I began to realize that what a teacher does not talk about comes across as a sign of disapproval. Friends talk about everything to each other. This parent was telling me that her child is Black and she wanted her difference in a White classroom talked about in natural ways.

SH: How did this experience change your work with children?

VP: In very important ways. I began to spend more time listening to myself as I talked to each child, listening to the child, and trying to make the connections between individual children and myself and myself and the group. Something made me realize I was missing much of what went on in that hidden curriculum—what it was that I hadn't heard, what had gone on in this complex relationship of children and children, and teachers and children, that I'd missed but that is crucial. These tiny incidents are what sometimes influence children for the rest of their lives, and it became something that I was fascinated by.

SH: In your book, *The Girl with the Brown Crayon,* you say it took you years to learn what your role as teacher was. How would you describe that role, and how did you discover it?

VP: Well, as I watched and listened to the children, I saw that their sense of inventiveness was greater than mine—mine was far more ordinary, far more conventional. And I began to take the children's invented stories, either in play or in dictation, as my starting point. The degree of concentration, the degree of focusing on their part in these stories, came across to me as being filled with such passion. I knew there must be some deep reason and that I must understand it. With this understanding, my role changed to more of a connection-maker than a lecturer.

Before this, I was certainly an adequate teacher, but the teaching plans emerged from my weekly plan book, teacher guides. For a long time I was mimicking things I remembered, but there was no sense that I was inventing something that reflected myself. My teaching lacked passion. I did see passion in the children's play, but it took me years to start reflecting on what I was doing. Then I began to seek a way that the passion in the children's play could be transferred to a passion for school, that connections could be made between their play and their learning. The children's stories then led to my own stories and gave me the rebirth in my classroom life that I needed. To say this sounds as if I simply changed overnight, but of course that was impossible. This was a long process, as any change is and must be. It took a lot of thinking about it. It really took me about 10 to 12 years to begin having some objectivity about who I was and what we were doing in the classroom.

SH: Looking back through those first 12 years, were there mistakes you made that you regret?

VP: I wouldn't regret any mistakes. Mistakes are essential to progress, yours or the children's. You can't avoid them. However, if you begin to keep a daily journal, you'll realize you can't really analyze the stuff that has gone well. What's to analyze? It's gone well through some kind of magic that's happened. What you can analyze are the errors. This is the great, good thing about things not going well and writing about them. Imagining doing things in another way, coming back the next day and the next week and continuing to try them another way. Then getting to the point where you can say to the children, "You know, I didn't like the way that activity went yesterday. Let's talk about it. Here is the sort of thing I didn't like—how about this? What didn't you like about it?" So I would say the whole point is that mistakes are essential. Study them, talk about them to the children, see if things go better when you try different things.

The children love figuring out how to do something in a different way. That's what their play is all about. They do it one way this day, and the next day they do it in an entirely different way. They keep putting on different disguises. They keep taking different roles. They see no reason not to. One day you're a baby—the next day you're a superhero. That's the way life goes. Try it all out. That's the natural way; and, in a sense, though they may not articulate it, when the play goes in an entirely different way the next day or the next, it's because they're trying to self-correct.

SH: You mentioned earlier that you eliminated the use of teaching guides. Can you tell us more about this?

VP: I think that once I discovered that the children themselves offered me what I needed to grow as a teacher, I doubt that I ever referred to teaching guides again; but looking back, it could be that I needed to start out that way. I certainly am not second-guessing a period of time that led me to begin to understand what was missing. Maybe I wouldn't have changed my path if I hadn't started in the first way and felt, quite frankly, the boredom of what I was doing.

It's enough to know that for this most complex of professions—teaching—one should expect a long period of self-training and analysis. I find you can't trust your memory. Keep track, write for yourself daily. You might want to use a tape recorder. That's what I did. Anyone who wants to become a writer about their classroom, as I have, has to have some means of keeping an absolutely accurate record all the while they're putting out fires in every part of the classroom.

SH: Did you have tape recorders set up in different places in the room?

VP: Never. I never used more than one tape recorder—it was never out of my immediate hearing, and I never used more than one cassette. Let me tell you why. Number one, this was a way of disciplining myself. I used only one cassette so that it had to be transcribed before I could use my tape recorder the next day. I felt there was absolutely no way I was going to collect a week's worth of tapes and give myself a whole weekend to work on them. That was unrealistic. Second, and more importantly, is that when I transcribed every day, I could bring back with great immediacy the errors and misconceptions and wonderful curiosities that I heard. Then I could say the next day, "John, when I listened to the tape recorder, I realized that I didn't hear your whole statement so what I told you was only for the first part." Of course, if you keep doing that for a period of over a year, you have your curriculum in logic and language built right there. But the most important reason I didn't have tape recorders placed around the room is this: If you leave a tape recorder playing unattended, there is an ethical problem—you are eavesdropping into conversations when you yourself are not there. I believe it is almost like putting a bug somewhere.

And everything is context, you see. If I am not there, I don't know the context in which everyone is speaking. I don't know if something is pretend or not pretend. I wouldn't see the face of the speaker, the response of people walking by. I wouldn't see someone giving someone a poke, either, or knocking over something.

In the classroom I'm recording life as it goes on while I am there. The children understand it perfectly well. They respect it. It means you are studying them. You are so enamored and respectful of who they are and what they think that you are compelled to study their work as if it's pure gold. That's a very respectful thing to do.

SH: Respect was the word I thought of when you were talking about asking students what they really said. That must give them a very strong sense of being valued.

VP: Oh, absolutely—and let's not forget since we're talking about education—you must value the power of the word. Words mean something. If it takes a whole week to figure out the meaning of a sentence, that's time well spent. I've come back 3 days in a row with the same question. Why not? That's a lesson we never forget for the rest of our lives. What exactly did a person mean? The way the meanings of words come across through the intense need to understand exactly what is being said, is never boring. It's never boring to talk about what you yourself have said, especially if you are a child and most people don't listen to you.

You yourself are saying, "I wonder why I said that?" You are scrutinizing yourself too. "That didn't come across the way I wanted it to"—which is true of so much of our conversations with each other. That's all right. You're not strangers passing in the night. You can keep correcting every day that you see each other.

SH: With this process, you are also teaching them to evaluate their own performance and words and actions; so they reflect too.

VP: Yes. And they know that all is not lost if you behave in a way that you're not proud of. It can be made up. That's what we do with each other. That's how we learn, because in a sense you keep reliving situations.

SH: Your teaching practice is unique. Were you supported by administrators and others in your work?

VP: I think it would be fair to say this: To the extent that I sought support, I would say I was supported. However, my intense preoccupation in the classroom and in my writing really did not allow many people to enter my sphere of reference. The children, parents, my co-teachers in the classroom—they really formed my support group. Had I sought more support and involvement, probably it would have been a good thing and I would have gotten it, but it wasn't the way I worked.

SH: At times our readers feel overwhelmed and frustrated by the demands of teaching. Were there times in your career when you felt overwhelmed, and how did you pull through those times?

VP: Yes. There were such times and I learned very quickly, some inner sense cautioned me, to pull back, that I was not someone who can handle too much stuff at once. I simply lessened the workload. I went to fewer meetings. I lessened the workload in the classroom too; and there was more time for play. More time for walks or outdoor times, or we would concentrate on some ongoing project that would bring us all together. Here was my reasoning: Nothing was going to come across well if I was all out of sorts and rushed. What overwhelmed me was too much stuff to do. I could tell when I started to become impatient with children that I needed to simply pull back and do more stories, spend more time reading, playing.

I can remember explaining this to a parent at an open house. "Why aren't you doing this? Why aren't you doing that?" I would say, "You know, I'm not a person who can do everything at once, and I suspect most of you aren't either. But since I want a happy and relaxed environment here, a culture built upon children who are learning to love school, I'm just not going to do the stuff that gets me overwhelmed until it comes at a more natural time." And I never had a parent who didn't say, "Great! Thanks for explaining it to me."

SH: You are a mentor for many teachers through your books. Did you have a mentor, and can you give an example of when you learned something from a mentor?

VP: I never had an official mentor, but I'll give an example of two people who had a great effect upon me. One was a science teacher and one was a special education teacher. They showed me what curiosity looked like in the teaching process. I met the science teacher after half a dozen years in my teaching. He came around once in a while just for the fun of it. That was the point. He wanted to see how young children think. You see, he had great curiosity. The other, in the next decade, was a special education teacher. Each of them glowed with excitement as they watched the thinking of their students. They just wanted to know how a child thinks and they were asking different sorts of questions to give the child a chance to reveal this. I learned a lot from those two people, watching them.

SH: A number of our readers are singularly impressed with your methods of research and how thoroughly you document the words of students and others involved in your classroom. Can you tell us how you do this and how you keep track of the data you collect?

VP: How do I keep track of it? Let me explain. You know these spiral notebooks—70 sheets in each one? I have dozens of them. I date the transcriptions, day by day. I use black ink and blue ink so I can tell my transcribed taped material from my commentary. It's a running commentary. Everything is dated. I will go back and forth—every page is numbered with the date at the top so that I can say, "Refer to Book 6, page 14." When I begin writing a book, I take out another color ink—red perhaps—and circle everything that pertains to the subject of the book. I date that. In other words, it is my own data but I take no chances of losing it even though I myself have written it down. You yourself must know what the context, the reference, is. I keep notes—"remember when so-and-so walked in," "this is before the birthday party . . ."

SH: Having recently retired, will you give more time to writing?

VP: Actually, it is hard to say that I have retired, though I no longer go to a classroom. I do travel throughout the world now. I'm still collecting data with my tape recorder, keeping track of my thinking with my daily journal because I'm always in the middle of a new book. I'm in the middle of one right now. It's too early to describe the contents, but I think it will be more of a spiritual journey than my other books. Maybe this is a result of my not pursuing the day-to-day responsibilities of teaching and everything that goes with it.

And, yes, wherever I go, my tape recorder is with me. I take my notebooks—I transcribe them early in the morning and late at night in the hotel room. So I think I probably will never lose this necessary connection— the teachers I talk to have the same kinds of questions as the ones you just presented to me. Some are very specific about incidents in their classrooms. But they want to bring up situations that puzzle them and to hear those situations talked about. Very often lately they have to do with the problem of inclusion or problems of not feeling comfortable with certain ways in which children and parents are reacting. And I will say, "Can't I meet with you someplace in the afternoon or after lunch and tape a discussion with you?" I still keep that going. Sometimes I may not have any use for it except simply for thinking. It's my way of continuing to reflect. You don't learn things well enough the first time around. You and I could have had this conversation well enough without a tape recorder and without your taking notes, and you could hang up and write something about it pretty well. But now you have your transcription of the tape; everything will be rethought as you put it down in a usable script.

SH: Could you talk more about inclusion?

VP: Well, I think it is a brand-new subject in a sense. After these legislative rulings that created integration, people are again almost beginning from scratch with a lot of consternation and conflict and yet a higher level of thinking and honest discussion about integration issues. So I think inclusion—in terms of minority groups, non-English-speaking groups, behavioral and learning differences, language differences, emotional differences, whatever—this is the new subject to be studied. And it must be studied classroom by classroom, by individual teachers, not just research people doing a Ph.D. study. Whoever can contribute some knowledge on this subject will be doing everyone a favor. Material has to be gathered. We have to know from little towns and big cities. How does it work? What works better than something else? What are the problems? I can tell from conversations that none of us know the dimensions of the problem. And more and more teachers must write for each other because if we just talk to each other, then only a handful of people hear.

We must transmit our experiences on this subject to one another, because there are many aspects to it. The list, which includes bilingual education, is enormous. I can only say, "Study that, study it for yourself. Deal with it for yourself. There are no curriculum plans or lesson plans. Invent your own way of dealing with it. Every child is different and has his or her own story to tell. You must be the scribe who tells it."

SH: Is there anything else you would like to say?

VP: I want to say that the questions coming from your readers have been excellent. I've really enjoyed talking about them and about other questions that came up. I feel as if I have had a discussion right now with all the people you talk to.

I must say I'm pleased and honored that such an excellent journal as *Foxfire*, with such a reputation for integrity, wanted to talk to me. You are a connection-maker, and there aren't many such journals around.

THE TEACHER AS MORAL
AND PHILOSOPHICAL GUIDE

The three interviews in Part III look at the inner lives of teachers, the importance of continuous moral self-evaluation, and serving as moral role models.

Chapter Eight

MAXINE GREENE

"I'm Pursuing Something I Haven't Caught Yet"

Maxine Greene is an outstanding and prolific American philosopher of education. A pioneer who has published numerous articles and books, including *The Dialectic of Freedom*, this long-time friend of Foxfire holds the William F. Russell Chair in Foundations of Education at Teachers College, Columbia University, where she began teaching in 1965. With a strong interest in aesthetic education, Greene has taught a course at Teachers College called Aesthetics in Education, a subject on which she continues to lecture and lead workshops at the Lincoln Center for the Arts in Education. She also has taught courses in the philosophy and history of education, social philosophy, and literature. She has lectured widely at universities and educational associations throughout the United States and abroad.

Her writings include books and many journal articles and chapters in essay collections, including: *The Public School and the Private Vision* (1965), *Existential Encounters for Teachers* (1967), *Teacher as Stranger: Educational Philosophy for the Modern Age* (1973), *Landscapes of Learning* (1978), *The Dia-*

[*Editor's Note*: As noted earlier, this interview was conducted by Lacy Hunter, one of the senior editors of *The Foxfire Magazine*, during her senior year at Rabun County High School, Rabun County, Georgia.]

lectic of Freedom (1988), *Releasing the Imagination: Essays on Education, the Arts, and Social Change* (2000), and *Variations on a Blue Guitar: The Lincoln Center Lectures on Aesthetic Education* (2001).

Greene has served as president of the American Educational Research Association and the Educational Studies Association. Her many honors include the 1992 John Dewey Society Award, Lifetime Achievement Awards from AERA and the Association of Colleges for Teacher Education, Barnard College's Distinguished Scholar Award, and several honorary degrees.

Interview—Fall 1996

LH: You probably know that at Foxfire we have a lot of respect for teachers' memorable learning experiences and the ways that thinking about them can inform a teacher's own teaching practice. Can you tell us about one of your own?

MG: Probably one of my primary learning experiences was when I was teaching one summer in Hawaii. I was doing a seminar—I think it was on history of American education—and it suddenly occurred to me that there was something about the way American imaginative writers like Hawthorne, Melville, Mark Twain, Scott Fitzgerald, and so on, looked at the culture and the way educators like Horace Mann looked at the culture. American artists always saw the kind of tragic dimension in American history when the industrial revolution began. So I thought, if I teach American history, I have to teach it from both perspectives: the Hawthorne, Twain, Scott Fitzgerald perspective and the Horace Mann, Dewey, Bonner perspective. So I have been doing that over all these years, and I wrote the book about it.

I have another learning experience with respect to the same thing. About 4 years ago, I suddenly realized that when I wrote the book *The Public School and the Private Vision*, I had thought that I was writing about adversary voices. It never occurred to me that I was using the old White man's tradition. I included a little Ralph Ellison, but now in my classes we read Frederick Douglass, we read Toni Morrison. I didn't have any women in that book because it was a different time, and now I hope to rewrite the book to include some of the people and voices I learned about so late.

That's one example of the kind of thing that has affected my teaching and affected me, and sort of made life worth living. Because I'm pursuing something I haven't caught yet.

LH: How do the lessons you took from it inform your work?

MG: Well, I believe that teaching involves a creation of situations— learning situations—in which people are moved to release and ask their own questions, then move beyond and think in terms of the unexplored, of what is possible and not just of what's predictable. And I try to teach in such a way as to give people the feeling that I don't come in with answers to the questions, that I am as open to questioning as they, my students, are. And what I am trying to make contagious is a sense of wonder, a sense of openness, a sense of curiosity, a sense that nothing is settled, that there is always something beyond.

That is the egalitarian in me, the person who is obsessed with imagination. I want to make subject matter—with the disciplines like history, literature, the sciences—sort of lenses that people can look through as they keep asking their own questions.

LH: Was there a moment when you knew that you were a teacher?

MG: Yes, I guess so, but I had never, ever thought of being a teacher. I had wanted to be a writer. I went to Barnard College, which is a women's college, and I found out, after being there 3½ years, that I had enough honor points to graduate or to leave. So I left and said to hell with this. I mean, I had enough points to have my degree. And nobody said, "Did you ever think of going to graduate school?" They just said, "Good-bye, Charlie." I think they thought that they educated us for marriage, civility, and philanthropy.

So I eloped right away with a doctor, and I had a child and I had jobs, and so on. Then I was divorced about 7 years later, and I remarried and went out to a housing suburb. I had a little daughter who was about 6 and was very upset by the divorce. So I went to her teacher and said, "Oh, you know, there has been a divorce and Linda's very upset." She said, "If she were my child, I would take a baseball bat to her." And I always tell people that that was where my career began. I thought, I can't have her in this school, so I had to drive her back to Brooklyn every day to her old school.

Then I thought, well, maybe I will go back to school. So I wrote to every university, asking could I be a special student. I had one criterion. The class had to be between 10:00 and 2:00, when Linda was in school. The one that was most lenient was NYU. It was a class given by three professors twice a week, 4 hours each day, from 10:00 to 2:00.

So I took that class, which was in philosophy of education and history, and they made me their assistant. Then they gave me a class to teach, believe it or not, my second year. One hundred and fifty people attended The History of Education at NYU. And that's when I realized that it is really a challenging, exciting thing to do if you can move just one person to live with more wonder and curiosity and imagination in pursuit of meaning. That's when I found out I was a teacher. I found out recently that Frank McCourt took my first class and actually felt affected by it. Remarkable!

LH: Many teachers who read our journal may at times feel overwhelmed and frustrated by the challenges that they are facing. Were there times in your own teaching or school work when you had those kinds of feelings?

MG: Of course—even today when I'm retired but still teaching, lecturing, and writing.

Society bears down so hard on the helpless and does so little for people who are poor and/or come from different places and are made to feel so unwelcome. One of the challenges is that it is a very unfair and unjust society that hasn't realized the promise of democracy. It is very hard for teachers to do much about that.

The challenges in schools are, How do you help the children learn to engage with disciplines with a sense of urgency? How do you bring art into the school? Those are educational challenges, but I think we are continually wounded by what lies around us. If the society was more child-oriented and cared more about children, it wouldn't be so tough.

LH: What are the things that motivated you and pulled you through the difficult times?

MG: Part of it was that I believed we could change things and make them better. I still think the high point in my life was in the 1960s. I wasn't a youthful person, but I was very much part of the peace movement and part, in my own way, of the Civil Rights Movement. The ideas of being committed to something, to move with other people even to make small transformations, are what pulled me through to the wonderful moments.

For example, I have some contact with the teachers in the New Visions schools in New York, which are small magnet schools that are being developed with the help of grants. When teachers get together on a particular theme—a particular commitment—you feel sort of hopeful. Some of the Foxfire ideas, when they began working—working in a small city school, say—often upset feelings of hopelessness and opened unexpected perspectives. People begin to reflect on their own lives or on their parents' stories or on local history or local traditions. Those are openings, and that's what pulls you through—a sense of possibility.

LH: Many of our readers are teachers who talk about experiencing a sense of isolation and the lack of support for the learner-centered, active classrooms that they try to create. In your teaching or school work, have there been times when you have experienced that isolation and lack of support?

MG: Well, I think it is very different in a university than in a school. It is very hard to find colleagues in a graduate school. If you are lucky you can. My best connection seems to be my students. Very often when students come over to the house or we go out for lunch, that is where I find my support.

LH: Is there some practical advice that you can give to those teachers out there who are in that kind of situation?

MG: I think today there is much more recognition of the need for community and the need for collaboration in public schools. And I think it is possible now.

When I was younger I sort of thought, if I close the door I can do anything, and I don't want anybody in here messing around with my business. But I know now the best thing is when teachers can come together and talk about their work together, share their experiences, their responses to children and children's journals.

One place where I've seen this work is called El Puenta, in Brooklyn. El Puenta means "The Bridge," and it's a center bridging the school, the community, the hospital, and the home, and advocating for freedom and democracy. The students are largely from South America. Among other things, the teachers make part of their curriculum a campaign for immunization in the neighborhood to be sure children are vaccinated against smallpox and to help the parents understand the immunization process. The children come together within their community and it becomes part of their social studies. This commitment by the teachers creates community, and that is so much better than remaining isolated behind a closed door.

LH: Are there things you have seen that encourage you or give you hope about the way teachers are doing their work with learners?

MG: Oh, yes. I know it's not nationwide, but I think it's one aspect of the school renewal movement today. Again, it may not be the whole country, but there is far more talk and far more thinking about active learning and the community. I'm speaking of the relation between learning and social action and the concerns for social justice and a recognition of the consciousness of different children. For example, I think the whole language movement is very encouraging. I think our interest in children's stories and journals and storytelling and opening to various kinds of experience are all things that give me hope.

LH: Of all that you have done in your career, which things have given you the greatest sense of pride or satisfaction?

MG: It's when somebody meets me in the park, or when I'm with my husband, and they say, "Her class changed my life" or "made me see differently." Or it's when I get a letter about a book I wrote, or people say, "You have really got me going." That's what makes a teacher feel pride—that you meant something to someone, either by your writing or your speaking or mostly by teaching. People say, "I remember you. You were my teacher 6 years ago." That's wonderful to me.

LH: Are there other things that you would like to say to our teacher-readers about the work of teaching?

MG: For me there is nothing more fascinating, nothing more life-affirming, because teaching, again, is an open-ended kind of undertaking. You never really know if you are successful. You are working with human possibility. You are trying to awaken people and overcome what Dewey used to call the "anesthetic" in life, the numbness. You are doing what Paulo Freire talks about when he talks about overcoming silences and giving people the capacity to overcome whatever internalized oppression they feel.

You can't promise anything by your teaching, but you can open doorways. You need enough confidence, somehow, in the human psyche to believe that people will walk through the doorways—if you can open them—and see all tentative realities.

So I guess that's what I would say. It may sound sentimental, but I believe it.

LH: In that vein, what words of encouragement and hope can you offer to our readers through their teaching right now?

MG: Only that they are part of a process, part of an opening. They're not in a product-oriented profession. They are in a process-oriented profession. They are helping people become different; they are helping people find their way. And in helping other people find their way, the teacher is in some way finding her way. I am an existential philosopher. I believe that we create our selves—our identities—by our projects. By choosing a project, which in my case is teaching and writing, I am creating a certain kind of identity. But I never finish. Old as I am, I still feel unfinished.

I think when you are a teacher, that's part of what you get out of it. You are in a world of incompleteness, and you are always reaching beyond where you are—the way you are helping young people reach beyond where they are. And that's the greatest gift that you can get, it seems to me.

LH: Mrs. Greene, all the senior editors, right now, of *The Foxfire Magazine* happen to be young women, and we understand that you were one of the first women in higher education. Can you tell us a little bit about what that was like?

MG: I really can't say I was one of the first, but when I went into the philosophy of education, there were very, very few women doing that.

In addition, the one woman philosopher of education whom I met while going to NYU was actually unable to see how you could combine doing philosophy in a man's world with having children and having a house. She said a terrible thing: She said I had to choose between being a woman and being a professor.

I chose being a professor—and I did go into philosophy. Not only that, but because I was always interested in literature, and because philosophy then was dominated by a kind of analytical linguistic approach, they used to say I was "soft," and that I was "afflicted by sobbing." I was "too literary," and that meant that I was too female.

It was difficult, but then I guess I was lucky. For one thing, I started publishing kind of early and would volunteer papers to my professional organizations. They took them, even though a lot of people, I suppose, didn't like what I said.

They eventually accepted my papers at the Philosophy of Education Society. I may have been doing what other people weren't doing—I was using literature and philosophy and talking about social issues. Eventually, I became president of that society, to my great surprise.

I was asked to go to Teachers College to edit the *Teachers College Record*. When I got there, I found out the Philosophy and Social Sciences Department had never hired a woman. So I was in the English Department at Teachers College for 5 or 6 years. I have an idea that one reason they took me into Philosophy and Social Sciences was that Donna Shalala (who was, you may recall, Secretary of Health and Welfare in the Clinton Administration) was hired by Teachers College. She came with lots of grants and lots of reputation. Then it was harder to keep a woman out.

Diane Graham—who later became head of the National Institute of Education, then Dean at the Harvard Graduate School of Education, then president of the Spencer Foundation—was also there. During those years, she and I were both allowed to teach one course in the Philosophy and Social Sciences Department and to attend its meetings. But we weren't accepted as full members. Finally, after Donna came, I was made part of the department. It was a long, uphill climb. Today I can look back and see much more than I saw when I thought it was all directed against me, personally. You know, not me as a woman, but me, personally.

LH: How have you seen things change for women?

MG: They've changed a great deal, partly because of feminism, but probably more important in our field, because of the recognition of a very significant scholarship in women's studies, feminist theory, ethics, and so on. These have gone on to affect philosophy and social thought generally.

The fact is that silent voices and all sides are being heard. That is due as much to the Feminist Movement as to the Civil Rights Movement. As bad as our times are, it's part of the great revolution of our times that women's voices are heard and minorities' voices are heard. And not only are they heard, they're changing the way people look at the world. Now, against every obstacle, we have to struggle to keep all that alive.

Chapter Nine

NEL NODDINGS

Teaching: A Lifelong Moral Quest

Nel Noddings has spent 15 years as a teacher, administrator, and curriculum developer in public schools. She served as a mathematics department chairperson in New Jersey and as Director of the Laboratory Schools at the University of Chicago.

Presently the Lee L. Jacks Professor of Education, Emerita, at Stanford University and Professor of Philosophy and Education at Teachers College, Columbia University, she is past president of the Philosophy of Education Society and the John Dewey Society.

In addition to 12 books—among them, *Caring: A Feminine Approach to Ethics and Moral Education*, *Women and Evil*, *The Challenge to Care in Schools*, *Educating for Intelligent Belief or Unbelief*, and *Philosophy of Education*—she is the author of more than 175 articles and chapters on various topics ranging from the ethics of care to mathematical problem-solving.

She is president of the National Academy of Education and a Laureate member of Kappa Delta Pi, and holds two honorary degrees in addition to a number of awards, among them the Anne Rowe Award for contributions to the education of women (Harvard University), the Willystine Goodsell Award (AERA), a Lifetime Achievement Award from AERA, and the Excellence in Education Award (Pi Lambda Theta).

Noddings and her husband enjoy living on the New Jersey shore and "having our kids and grandchildren for the summer."

Interview—Winter 2000

SH: Can you tell us about a memorable learning experience you had as a student?

NN: As a kid and all through college, everything came very easily to me; I was disgusted if I got anything below 95. At one point in high school, I became bored with American history because the teacher was going over stuff that I thought people should have learned in eighth grade. So the teacher did something that was really quite wonderful. He said, "OK, why don't you read this book?" and he gave me a historical novel by Kenneth Roberts entitled *Oliver Wiswell*, and I read that book and was just astonished. Even today, when I think back on it, I think of it as an incredible experience, because I realized about halfway through it that if I had been alive during Revolutionary War days, I probably would have been a Tory. I can remember walking up and down the beach talking to myself about this possibility, because the Tories seemed to be more loyal, steadfast, thoughtful, reasonable people. I felt like a traitor to my own country a couple of hundred years later. Right after that he gave me Charles Beard's *An Economic Interpretation of the Constitution of the United States*, and I was somewhat disillusioned about the founding fathers, though enlightened.

So this learning experience really stands out for me. It made me think. It made me realize that you've got to dig beneath the surface of things and mull it over, be reflective, really think about it.

The second one would be termed a negative experience. When I was working for my master's in mathematics, I finally had trouble with a course. It was a brand-new experience. I was taking about four courses, and this one was sort of the straw that broke the camel's back. At the time, my father was dying, my mother was understandably in a terrible state, my sister was sick, and I had five little kids at home. At first, because I wasn't aceing this course, I thought there was something wrong with me. I agonized over it, and decided that this obviously wasn't the field for me because I couldn't hack the course. How is it a learning experience? It really changed the way I looked at students and the challenges they face. I learned that people are very different and go through very different experiences, and teachers ought to be sensitive to these experiences. So, much as I hated this experience, it was a very good one for me.

And I would add that what I learned as a mother was more valuable than all the things we've talked about because I saw firsthand that kids are very different and have very different interests.

SH: How did these experiences influence what you do with students?

NN: The high school experience encouraged me to think and, in turn, to encourage my students to think, not just hand back what the teacher wants. The second, and my years as a mother, made me more sensitive to the kinds of things students go through. All of these affected my writing and my teaching.

SH: Do you remember a significant learning experience you had as a teacher?

NN: Loads of them. One involves my first teaching experience. When I finished my bachelor's degree in mathematics, there just weren't any math jobs available, so I took a job teaching in a sixth-grade, self-contained classroom. I was nervous about it, but I absolutely loved it. It gave me an opportunity to revisit all the literature of my childhood, all the things I enjoyed so much in school. Then at the end of the year, we were asked if we would like to stay together for another year. So the kids and their parents had to write letters saying they were willing to do this—which was a good thing. I think these things should be decided by mutual consent. And so we stayed together for another year. At the end of that year, we were asked again if we wanted to stay together for still a third year; and so I stayed with those kids for 3 years.

I have never forgotten that experience, and it has been fundamental in so much that I have written and so much that I did afterward. Because when you have that kind of continuity, when you stay with kids for 3 years rather than one, you really get to know them and you contribute to their lives in ways that would be intrusive if you didn't know them as well.

The following year when I went into high school teaching math, I had the same experience. I took in lots of kids in the beginning of their high school math and took them right through their advanced placement calculus. It's an experience that I would recommend to every teacher. It taught me about the need for continuity, the need to be with kids and to really get to know them, to share with them, to give them opportunities to do things that fit with their own interests and talents.

SH: Do you remember mistakes you made as a teacher? Can you tell us if and how a mistake made a difference in your thinking about teaching?

NN: I still grieve over one from my beginning years as a math teacher—this was before that experience I had in graduate school. I was a very strict grader; I was very fair and always helped kids and all that, but I was a strict grader. I remember this kid who got a 13 on a major test, and she flunked the course. The mother came in to plead, and the principal backed me all the way. He said afterward that if I hadn't been such a strong teacher, he wouldn't have backed me. So here's this poor kid who flunked the class. Later, I thought, "This is not helpful." Anyone who knows just basic arithmetic knows you can't recover from a 13. You put a 13 in with two or three other grades and divide by three or four, and you've got a horrible grade, and there's no recovery from it. So a couple of years later when I really thought about that, I decided that I would never do that again.

So, after that, I told the kids in all my math classes that they all start at 50—it's not a good grade, but that's where you start—and you can only go upward from there. After that, I used a method of cumulative grading so kids could see how they were improving. I never again gave a grade as low as 13. I learned from that experience. And closely associated with never giving a grade under 50 was the notion of continuous progress—that at least in a subject like math, which is sequential, if kids don't know one batch of material, they really can't master the next. Watching that over a period of time, I finally decided that the thing to do was to have them take tests over again until they had mastered one thing before going on to the next. In a subject like math, it makes ultimate sense to me. If you want people to learn, you don't penalize them for their mistakes but you help them to learn it. Kids would say to me, "How many times can we take the test?" And I would say, "As many times as are available in the marking period," because the idea is to learn, not to be defeated by it.

I feel very strongly about grades. I hate giving grades. I think it gets in the way of the teacher–student relationship. When I taught at Stanford, I didn't have to give grades. Instead, students would write papers, and I would have them write them over again—sometimes more than twice—because we both wanted a satisfactory result. That was the object—to get a result that was satisfying to them and satisfactory to me and that didn't involve grades. I still feel very strongly about that.

SH: Did you have a mentor?

NN: Oddly enough, I really didn't. Certainly not before I went into doctoral work, and then I had a wonderful advisor; he was encouraging, and that was great. But he couldn't really help me get into the field the way some mentors do because his interests were quite different. So oddly enough, I can't really say I did have a mentor.

SH: Do you act as a mentor to students?

NN: I do. Yes. I mentor quite a few people. In fact, a few years ago I was delighted to get a Spencer Mentor Grant. It just came out of the blue. The Spencer Foundation gave a number of these very nice awards to a number of people around the country. I got it the second year of the program, and they've been doing it since. They give funds to several professors to use for student support. I used the grant money to hire students to work with me and to pay some of their travel expenses to conferences—it all went to student support.

SH: Looking back at your career, what are the things you've done that give you the greatest sense of accomplishment and satisfaction?

NN: I'm very happy about the reception of several of my books. I've been writing on the ethics of caring for several years now, and the reception of them has been quite satisfying. Certainly the success of my students has been satisfying. My own pleasure in the profession has been wonderful. In the words of one of my colleagues, "It's just the best job in the world." This is the way he put it. This was in response to some young people on the faculty who were groaning under the pressure. And they were right. When you're a professor at a major research university, you're under a major amount of pressure. So they were listing all their complaints and troubles. And he said, "You're right. Everything you've said is right. But it's just the best job in the world." And I agree with that. I think that's absolutely right.

SH: Can you think of a struggle or hard time that was particularly important to you?

NN: Well, certainly the struggle of grading has been an important one for me. I tell my students that teaching is a lifelong moral quest. You never have it exactly right, and you keep trying to get better at it. You keep learning from your students and what they're going through, how you can do things better. It would be hard to pick out one thing, but the struggle with grading has been fundamental for me. My other struggle has been to find ways to broaden my courses so that a wide range of interests is captured, making it possible for people with very different interests from the ones I have, to engage the subject matter and to satisfy the course requirements in somewhat different ways.

SH: You mentioned the work you do with the ethics of caring. I wonder if you could say something about your beliefs about connection to community.

NN: Actually, I think "care," as I've described it, is an attribute of relations in which the "carer" contributes in a distinctive way and the "cared for" contributes by recognizing the efforts of the carer. I think that's even more fundamental than community. The community built on that notion is likely to be inclusive, whereas communities without that can be exclusive. In a number of things I've written, I've pointed out that community is something that we all desire but it has a dark side as well as a bright side; and there have been communities that have been enormously damaging to people outside the community. They become sort of insular and arrogant and sometimes even harmful to people inside as well as outside the community, so that it seems to me communities have to be built upon relations of care. Otherwise, they can become quite dangerous.

SH: I'm reminded of something Jack Shelton said when I interviewed him. He said that ethics are not built in isolation.

NN: I think that's exactly right. The ethic of care is a thoroughly relational ethic. It emphasizes our moral interdependence and doesn't center on the individual moral agent. I often say to classes and audiences that how good I can be depends partly on how you treat me. We need to realize that. It isn't just a matter of a set of virtues in the moral agent. It's a matter of the whole climate to be built up in the kinds of relationships we establish.

SH: What is it in what you do that inspires you to keep working?

NN: It's a lot of things. One thing is freedom. There aren't many jobs in the world in which you can be really in charge of what you're doing, and that's one thing that's wonderful about professorial work. The second thing is I love the ideas that I work with and I don't seem to run out of them. More keep coming all the time, and that's wonderful—and then, of course, the people that I work with. I really like teaching, and I've never found it in conflict with my scholarship; I've always found the two to be synergistic. There just isn't very much bad about it. Most of it is exciting, except committee work.

SH: Is there anything you would like to say to teachers about teaching?

NN: I would really like to endorse much of what Foxfire is doing and has stood for. I have referred to Foxfire in a number of my articles and books, and the thing that I find most outstanding about the stories from the books is that kids are encouraged to remain attached to their geographic places and communities and yet grow in skills that enable them to communicate beyond. I'm doing some work now on place, which is becoming quite exciting both in education and philosophy, and this seems to me a place where Foxfire has made a real contribution—to the notion of place—because you don't want kids to think they're living in the backwoods or that they're living in the inner city or that they're living in some other place that they should get out of; and yet you want to give them the knowledge and skills that will permit them to do that if they want to do it. That is a really stellar contribution of Foxfire.

SH: Is there anything you would like to say to teachers?

NN: The most fundamental thing is to listen to your students. Listen to them and try to connect what you think they *should* learn with what it is they *want* to learn. And if you connect those two things, you're going to have a wonderful partnership with kids or students of any age.

Chapter Ten

PARKER J. PALMER

Seeking Creative Solitude and Community

Parker J. Palmer is a writer, teacher, and activist who works independently on issues in education, community, leadership, spirituality, and social change. His work spans a wide range of institutions: colleges and universities, public schools, community organizations, churches and retreat centers, corporations, and foundations. He serves as Senior Associate of the American Association of Higher Education, as Senior Advisor to the Fetzer Institute, and as founder of Fetzer's  "Teacher Formation Program" for K–12 teachers across the country.

Palmer's work has reached a wide audience, having been featured by the *New York Times*, the *Chronicle of Higher Education*, *Change Magazine*, the *Christian Century*, CBS-TV News, National Public Radio, and the Voice of America.

In 1998, the Leadership Project (a national survey of 11,000 faculty and administrators) named Palmer one of the 30 "most influential senior leaders" in higher education and one of the 10 key "agenda-setters" of the past decade: "He has inspired a generation of teachers and reformers with evocative visions of community, knowing, and spiritual wholeness."

His books include: *Let Your Life Speak: Listening for the Voice of Vocation* (2000), *The Active Life* (1999), and *The Courage to Teach: Exploring the Inner Landscape of a Teacher's Life* (1998). His writing has been recognized with six honorary doctorates, two "Distinguished Achievement" awards from the National Educational Press Association, an "Award of Excellence" from the Associated Church Press, and "Critics' Choice" citations from *Commonweal* and *Christian Century* magazines.

Palmer lives in Madison, Wisconsin. A grandfather, he particularly enjoys taking his granddaughter, Heather, fishing.

Interview—Fall 1998

SH: As you know, at Foxfire we believe that reflecting on another's memorable learning experience can inform our own practice. Can you recall a memorable learning experience that had a powerful impact on you and your work?

PP: My most significant learning experience was my journey with clinical depression. Clinical depression comes in different forms—from genetic to biochemical to situational—and needs to be treated accordingly. To deal with situational depression, which is what I had, I needed to address how I was living my life. It compelled me to do the deepest learning of all: learning about one's self, penetrating illusions about who one is and how one is related to the world, and finding the ground of reality as a new place to stand. The kind of depression I had forces you to come to terms with your own truth, your own nature, your gifts, and your limits—and forces you to be in the world and in your work in a way that's more congruent with your own true nature. It's either that or die. My kind of depression came from living with illusions, and the journey to wholeness or back to health was a journey through illusion to reality.

Now, the liberal arts tradition has always been about gaining self-knowledge, and it's a great tradition. But if you look at the experiences in which people gain self-knowledge, they are seldom in the classroom. They come through powerful life experiences. So I'm naming depression as my great learning experience because it helped me gain deep, painful, but ultimately healing self-knowledge.

This journey impacted my work and my life as a teacher in very important ways. I became myself, I think—and students have an easier time relating to a person who is himself rather than hiding out behind a role. My journey through depression made me more real, more present, less defensive, less guarded—all of which I regard as inward steps toward better teaching.

Out of this experience came a major theme of my work: "living divided no more." I believe powerful things happen when people make the decision to live divided no more—by which I mean, "I will no longer behave on the outside of my life in a way that contradicts truths I hold deeply on the inside." When a person makes that decision, they claim their own authenticity. And that was critical to me as a person and as a teacher.

It's critical to all teachers, I think. I don't believe a divided teacher can be a good teacher. In my book, *The Courage to Teach*, I argue that there is one thing that all good teachers have in common: They all have a "capacity for connectedness." They all connect their selfhood with their students and their subject. Good teachers weave a fabric of connectedness between all three, and the loom on which they do the weaving is their own heart. You cannot do that with a divided self. If you don't have a level of self-knowledge that helps you overcome the internal disconnections in your own life, you can't teach well.

We are trained in the academic community to disconnect ourselves from everything—that's what the cult of "objectivism" is all about. But when teachers do that, we are teaching students to be unhealthy, unwhole.

As I go around the country talking to students, I hear a common complaint: "My teachers never tell me why they care about a subject, so why should I care about it?" They are talking about teachers who are lost in this culture of disconnectedness, teachers who need to reconnect with their hearts, their passions. It's our capacity to teach our subjects out of our own authenticity that builds a bridge between the students—who are often fearful—and subjects that are often fearsome.

SH: In addition to dealing with depression, were there times as a teacher when you felt frustrated and overwhelmed by the challenges you faced in the classroom?

PP: Teaching is the most demanding thing I've ever tried to do, and I always feel overwhelmed by its challenges! Every time you go into a teaching and learning situation, so much is at stake—it is a deep and precious exchange between human beings. It's overwhelming sometimes the way fear, for example, dominates so many educational settings. It's frustrating the way questions of power and ego and just basic human relationships keep rising up and getting in the way of what we'd like to do in the classroom.

SH: Is there an example of a particularly frustrating time in your teaching, and what helped you through that difficult time?

PP: My difficult times in teaching are so frequent it is hard to choose one example! When I was a young teacher, I thought, "After a few years pass and I get more experience, it'll no longer be so hard." Well, I'll be 64 next year, and it's still difficult—and I mean that to be reassuring! It's good to know I can still feel the struggle after so many years; that means my heart is still open and alive, which is a key to good teaching. What helps me through hard times is my own spirituality, my sense that the worth of the human self goes beyond the work one does and how well that work is going.

For me, spirituality is all about finding a sense of self that does not depend on externals. It's about finding deeper ground on which to stand—where you have worth just by virtue of being you, of being the gift that you are. It's about finding ground on which to stand apart from the shifting sands of other people's opinions, or your own measurable "success."

SH: Were there times when you felt a sense of isolation and lack of support from other teachers and administrators?

PP: Yes. In fact, having prepared myself for a teaching career in the university by getting a Ph.D., I left academic life after 3 or 4 years because of these feelings. I felt very alone in the kind of values we've just been talking about—caring for students, passionate engagement between teachers, students, and subjects—things I cared about deeply but found that many of my colleagues did not. Or so it seemed to me at the time, in my youthful anger, despair, and self-righteousness! Today I might see more allies, more "closet carers," among my colleagues.

SH: So you dropped out of teaching?

PP: I either dropped out or dropped in, depending on how you look at it! I left my professorship at Georgetown University and went to a Quaker living/learning community called Pendle Hill, an adult study center where life is a daily round of common meals, worship, physical work, social service, decision-making by consensus, and studying together. I spent 11 years at Pendle Hill, five as dean of studies. There I found a community of support around the kind of things I valued in education. So yes, I left formal higher education, but I did so in order to go deeper with the kind of education I wanted to pursue. It was a wonderful and transforming period of my life. But it was also very demanding and scary, full of fears that I was going to get lost professionally. Looking back, I am very glad I went that way because that was what forced me to think differently about teaching and learning and to find a different way of engaging this profession.

SH: Do you have advice for other teachers who experience a similar sense of isolation and lack of support?

PP: Two things have been helpful to me in times of despair. One is to set aside regular time to search my heart, in silence—walking in the woods, maybe journaling, maybe reading a good novel or good poetry, whatever it is that will help me sense more clearly what's going on inside. Teachers who are in tough situations need some form of creative solitude to tap the wellsprings of their own courage and truth.

Secondly, we all need community—and since community is hard to come by in this society, we need to find ways of gathering it unto ourselves. In every situation where a person feels isolated because of their values, there will be two, three, four other people who also feel that way. Part of our task is to search out folks who are on this journey with us and gather them in various ways, creating communities that can help us follow our own lights and do the best work we can. When you're isolated, you truly believe those people aren't there. Maybe they aren't there at your school, though I bet they are! But I am sure they are there at a school down the road, or in a nearby church or synagogue, or somewhere within reach—people who share your values and struggle to keep them alive. We can always reach out and create a community of support—if we don't lose hope.

SH: Have you learned from other teachers?

PP: What I learned from great teachers is they believe in who they are. They're willing to make vulnerable their own sense of self, to share that self with others, to put themselves out there in risk-taking ways. I didn't learn methods to imitate from those great teachers. By modeling authenticity, they encouraged me to learn a way of being myself in the world, the particulars of which I needed to discover for myself.

SH: When you visit with teachers and look at the way they do their work with learners today, are there things you see that encourage you or give you hope for the future of teaching?

PP: Absolutely. There's a tremendous revival of concern about good teaching in higher education today that was not there 20 years ago. At that time, regard for good teaching was at a low ebb in colleges and universities, which place so much emphasis on research. It's encouraging to see that in all kinds of institutions—large and small, public and private—there's a recent rallying around good teaching. I'm less well acquainted with what is going on in public education, although for the past 8 years I've been helping the Fetzer Institute develop a wonderful thing called the Teacher Formation Program. [See *www.teacherformation.org*.] This is a 2-year program of quarterly renewal retreats for cadres of 25 K–12 teachers around the country, and it's been an amazing experience for me. I have learned so much about the remarkable people who are out there teaching in our schools. I take great heart from knowing the qualities and commitments they hold to in the midst of the sad plight of public education.

SH: What would you say to give them encouragement and hope?

PP: I would say, "The work you're doing is very important. Many of us value it much more deeply than comes across in the public arena." I would say, "Believe in yourself and believe in your vocation." This society sends out so many mixed messages about teachers and teaching. We depend very heavily on our teachers and on the excellence of their work—and yet we demean and devalue them. We ask them to solve all the social problems that no one knows how to solve—and then we lay a tremendous guilt trip on them for all their alleged inadequacies. So teachers have to learn to take care of their own souls, in solitude and community. The Teacher Formation Program offers such support for the teacher's soul. But teachers, like everyone else, must learn to give that to themselves—because they owe it to their souls and to the students they serve.

SH: Looking back at your career, what are the things you have done that give you the greatest sense of accomplishment and satisfaction?

PP: I've taught courses, led workshops, and written books and articles in which I take great satisfaction. But courses end and books go out of print. What lasts for me are the heart-to-heart encounters with many dedicated people, encounters that have been as encouraging to me as I hope they've been to them. Last week I heard from a woman who teaches on a reservation in the southwest. The conditions in her school are painful, but a friend had given her *The Courage to Teach* and she's getting up an hour earlier every morning to read it in a slow, meditative way—which is giving her strength to go on with the important work she's doing. When I get a call like that, it's not just that my book touched a human life, but that a human life reached out to touch my own. I think that's the greatest reward of all— especially when it comes from a situation where I know that I would not have what it takes to be a teacher. It's a miracle to me that somehow, something I wrote would be supportive of that courageous woman in that difficult situation.

SH: Did you have a mentor?

PP: I've been blessed with many mentors. In my twenties, thirties, even forties there was always an older person who gave me the sort of support and guidance I needed. One is a man named Bob Lynn, who was vice president of the Lilly Endowment, which generously supported some of my early writing. But beyond the financial support, Bob was the person who would sit me down and help me find out what I really cared about and then say to me, "If you care about it that much, you need to write about it so you can share that caring with others."

As I approached my fifties, I realized my task in life was to turn around to younger people and offer them the same support and caring I've received from elders. I've been actively trying to do that—and there are many younger colleagues for whom I am glad to serve as a mentor. It's a gift you keep by giving it away.

SH: Can you describe the value this has for you?

PP: As you grow older, if you do not stay connected with the younger generation, you lose something of tremendous importance in life. When the younger and older generations become disconnected, it's like disconnecting the poles of a battery—you lose the flow of life-giving energy. For me, mentoring younger people keeps the energy flowing. I think I have something to give them because of my experience, and I know they have a lot to give me because they inhabit a world I don't fully understand. They encourage me because they remind me that the values I care about are not dead but are very much alive in the hearts of certain young teachers, scholars, and activists.

SH: In *The Courage to Teach*, you write of teachers experiencing despair concerning institutional impediments to reform and you speak of seeing those impediments positively. Can you explain this for our readers?

PP: The last chapter, "Divided No More: Teaching from a Heart of Hope," is based on a study I've done of social movements and how they evolve. I looked at the Civil Rights Movement, the Black Liberation Movement, the Women's Movement, the Movements for Freedom in Eastern Europe, Latin America, and South Africa—places where the obstacles to truth and justice were at least as formidable as they are in education! What's most interesting about those movements is that they start not with external social change strategies or techniques for manipulating institutions, but inside of people—in hearts and minds that have what I call a "movement mentality"—in people like Rosa Parks or Vaclav Havel, who led the liberation of Czechoslovakia.

This movement mentality arises as we experience institutional opposition—an experience many reform-minded teachers have as the educational institution rears up and says, "Stop! We're not going to let you go any further." There's something in people like Rosa Parks that—instead of receiving resistance as a sign of defeat, instead of throwing up their hands, and saying "OK, the game is lost"—internalizes that opposition as a sign that they are right! The opposition lets them know that the problem is exactly as big and deep and important as they thought it was—and there's something in this sort of turn of mind or alchemy of heart that takes these experiences that would otherwise be defeating and turns them into energy for change.

I think everybody who's ever taken leadership in a movement has had that kind of alchemy at work inside of them. It's important for all of us to find ways to become alchemists of our own experience so that when the institution says, "Stop!" we can say, "Well, that's clear evidence I'm on the right track. I must be doing something right—and I need to keep on doing it!"

TEACHING PLACE, FOSTERING CONSEQUENTIAL LEARNING

In Part IV, educators Jack Shelton and Bobby Ann Starnes reveal the great need to value and draw upon one's culture and to make learning meaningful within the context of a student's community.

Chapter Eleven

JACK SHELTON

Bringing Teachers, Students, and Community Together for Powerful Change

Jack Shelton, an advocate for rural communities, place-based education, and small schools, has made a significant contribution to the understanding of the importance of place and the value of schools as an agent for community-building. He recently retired as director of the Program for Rural Services and Research, which he organized in 1979 at the University of Alabama. He also founded the Student Coalition for Community Health and the PACERS Cooperative, an association of rural schools throughout Alabama, of which he was coordinator for 30 years.

A Lyndhurst Prize winner, he received his Ph.D. from the University of Glasgow, Scotland, and undergraduate and master's degrees from Birmingham Southern College and Duke University, respectively.

He has just completed a book entitled *Consequential Learning* in conjunction with the Kettering Foundation.

An ordained minister, Shelton lives with his wife, Martha, in his great-grandparents' house in Westover, Alabama. They have three sons and several grandchildren.

Interview—Winter 2000

SH: Can you tell us a memorable learning experience you had as a student?

JS: Yes, several tied to my experiences as a student in my hometown. I'm from a rural community, and through junior high school I went to a small rural school. Our school didn't have a lot of books, didn't even have indoor plumbing. But I kept noticing what happened to my classmates. My school was graduating kids who, by most theories at the time, were not supposed to be successful in business or as researchers or medical doctors or Ph.D.s or whatever. We weren't supposed to be able to do that; but by golly, that's what was happening all the time. I always took note of how important the community was for all of us, how important the school was. I knew everyone; everyone knew me; I had a place; I had responsibilities— most everyone did. We brought in the coal, cleaned the blackboards, swept the hall, or helped lime the baseball field. There was always something they called on us to do, and they always called us by name. I felt I was really accountable in my community.

When I was in sixth grade, we had a teacher who taught us how to make things—birdhouses and all kinds of things to give to someone, usually our mothers. The teacher also asked me to write and direct a play, which I did. We did our play and all of our parents and relatives came and we gave them the things we had made for them. That was a terrific experience for me.

SH: How did this later affect your work?

JS: I think I've gone back to it a lot without even thinking about it. Certainly what we did in PACERS reflected that. We worked from the knowledge that it's important for kids to have an opportunity to do something that makes a difference in their community. For example, if a group of kids in a PACERS school chooses to produce a community newspaper, they are doing something that affects the overall well-being of their community, which didn't have a resource for documenting community life. When they do that kind of work, they have an audience; but more importantly, they're changing the place where they live. That relates to what we were doing in sixth grade. It wasn't just that our parents saw us in our play or that they got something we made. The important thing was they took the birdhouse each of us made home and put it on the shelf or hung it in the yard— something was done that affirmed the kids and changed a little bit the relationship between us and our parents.

SH: Can you tell us about a memorable learning experience you had as a teacher?

JS: For a long time, I taught courses related to issues that affect rural people, especially in Alabama. One year I gave a lecture on how hard it is just getting around in rural places because of the fact that we don't have public transportation. Some of my students said, "Let's do the math." They wanted to do math tracing the change in the availability of public transportation from 1940 to 1960 to 1980. They researched airlines, buses, and trains. And they just kept on working way beyond any course requirements. They would come to my office and use the phone, use our information, and go places and interview people; and what we came up with was some very impressive information on social change in rural Alabama. I learned that when you see the opportunity to really apply academic skills to something, it's not abstract or meaningless but can really benefit someone. That is powerful.

SH: Did that change your thinking?

JS: It validated something I had already decided but had not fully realized or articulated. I already understood the need for education to be active, and I understood the need for students to feel as if they are educating themselves—to get all the tools and skills they need. Even before coming to the university, a lot of my work was heading in that direction. I was a campus minister for a long time at the University of Alabama, and I got students together and we set up projects from helping farmers to market food to setting up shelter homes for kids adjudicated delinquent who otherwise were going to jail. I had been involved with students taking responsibility for a very long time. What I hadn't had was that sort of academic framework where kids connected their academic interests with beneficial outcomes they generated. That experience not only confirmed my own earlier academic understanding; it also confirmed that we could get students at any level interested in the application of academic skills whenever they saw a beneficial outcome. I found students work especially well together when something is at stake like that. That was really meaningful. I had seen that outside the context of the classroom, but I hadn't seen it a lot *in* the classroom.

SH: Can you tell me about your work with PACERS and why and how your organization moved to work with teachers?

JS: When I think about the founding of PACERS, I think back on the fact that those of us who started it had one thing in common: We all came from or knew well small rural schools. We knew they had unrecognized strengths. We knew we wanted to build on those similar strengths in the rural communities we were to work with and that was to be the background of our work.

We also came to realize that the central resource in any rural community was the school. You can't do or sustain much that doesn't involve the school. In order to do what we said we were going to do—which was to help rural communities through a variety of partnerships to improve their circumstances—we knew we had to work in and with schools in partnership. Perhaps most important, we were interested in how we could get public work done collaboratively with teachers. We went to the school because we knew there were people in the institution who were really capable. I stress that because we never had a charity approach to what we were doing. These schools, teachers, and kids were our partners. When we went into the schools, we believed everyone was equal—no one was better than anybody else and no one knew any more than anyone else—each person just knew different things.

SH: What role did you see teachers taking in that process?

JS: In my mind, a school that is not a part of the community does not fully exist; it's almost an abstraction. I think for the school's own benefit, it needs to be engaged with the place where it exists; and it needs to use the tools and strengths it has in that place to make a difference there. There are professionals in the school. Often the school has the biggest local budget and most of the informational resources. In the schools we worked with, when they began to engage in their communities, they got so much back.

It is very much a matter of self-interest. For example, if kids in a community decide to publish a newspaper, the engagement of the community in those schools is so much higher, and the community's awareness of the schools is very much greater. The kids start spending time with the town councilmen and mayor in order to report what's going on. That's powerful interaction—it makes a difference in the town, and the schools ultimately benefit from it.

Teachers led this process, and, incidentally, the teachers began to overcome the role of being the importer of external information and then testing the random available memory of their kids. They started helping the kids become engaged in the community, and one of the things that happened was that the kids no longer just received the products of an academic discipline. For example, they didn't just read what a newspaper writer wrote, what a journalism textbook said; they went out and became the writer, the publisher. In turn, that enabled the teacher to take on a different role because she didn't *have* all the information they needed. She had to teach her kids how to use academic skills, how to do research, how to write for purpose; and she engaged other people to judge her students' work in a very direct fashion. Sometimes that scares teachers, but when they make such a change, it's powerful.

Instead of teaching kids information about science, she can teach the kid to *be* a scientist. She engages the student in *creating* the material. In other words, students *become* scientists, artists, musicians, playwrights, historians of their communities, publishers, and builders. The teacher can't do all that work, so she must *facilitate* kids gaining the necessary skills and applying those skills. Her role changes and becomes a lot more public. In my work, I saw a huge change in the way people taught. I heard a lot of folks say, "I used to be a teacher; now I coach."

SH: Did that happen after involvement with PACERS?

JS: Well, I think some of them are ready to do it, period. We just provided a way for them to do it by giving them such things as the money they needed, the authority they needed to venture out, opportunities to get together with other teachers where they could share and affirm their ideas. We prompted people to think beyond where they were and asked them to build on their strengths and use their imagination. We asked such questions as, "How can you relate what your kids learn to the place they live in, and what are the strengths in this community you can draw from?" There are a lot of questions like that, that will prompt teachers to do what they've always wanted to do.

That's how PACERS began. We went to all 30 schools and asked, "What do you do well? What do you think your strengths are? What are the strengths of this community? How can you build upon your strengths? How can you build upon your community's strengths? How can you create common ground between your school and community?" Those were our essential organizing questions for all our programs and approaches.

SH: Did you draw them into a discussion and then they directed the work?

JS: That's right. One of the things we were after was collaboration across the state. We didn't want isolation within a school; we didn't want isolation between a school and community. And we didn't want isolation between school, community, and other areas of the state. We asked teachers in a series of meetings the sort of raw questions I've given you. The second level was, "OK, having thought about your strengths and what you can do, put it on paper and share it with other teachers at the school and kids and community members. Then write a plan of what you want to do in your school, provided we can get the money or the authority to do that." Then we brought schools together in cluster meetings. We'd have four, five, six schools fairly close together geographically and everyone brought their plan and got up and read it to teachers and administrators and community people and students from other schools, which was very powerful.

After that we took all those plans—the schools modified them and brought them all together at a big statewide conference and laid them out on tables. We then spent a long time reading them. Then all the teachers and community members who wanted to help took the plans and determined what the common elements were of the various plans.

From this we got common approaches and a common agenda that was generated out of specific and individual communities and teacher interests. That has really worked well for us. It was a good way to organize an association of schools and teachers.

SH: You obviously have a strong moral and ethical code. How have you found a way to put that code into action in your work, and how can teachers "teach" a moral code to kids?

JS: I think it's less putting it into action than simply finding it. I'm convinced that the way kids come to ethical and moral formation, a sense of being part of their community, is for them to be known, to have responsibilities, and to be accountable for what they do. They have to pay the direct consequences of and get affirmed for what they do.

In big schools or schools not connected to place, kids may not have a role and they're anonymous, the teachers are anonymous, the places are anonymous. I don't believe morality is a function of anonymity. I'm always astounded at how few discipline problems small schools have. At one school, a principal had had to expel two students one year and he was bemoaning the fact—that was not supposed to happen there. It was almost traumatic for him. I think small schools connected to their places have a lot fewer discipline problems.

SH: What is it in what you did at PACERS and how you think about your work that inspired you then and now inspires you to work as an advocate and writer?

JS: Well, it's the impact that collaborative work has in the lives of teachers, students, and communities. I came in contact with teachers who, before their involvement with PACERS, were going to quit—teachers who had the skills and could do great work but for whom the overriding system in education did not engage their hearts or their minds very well. So one thing that was really rewarding for me was to see such teachers have a dream and get the chance—from collegial opportunities, financial support, and other kinds of opportunities created by PACERS—to address their dreams and then to see them complete their dreams.

There's a guy we work with who was and is a model for me in a lot of ways. He wanted an aquaculture unit for his kids. He's a VOC/AG teacher and he already knew what the science was he could teach kids and how they would learn if they were given responsibility. We knew his ideas had great potential but we just couldn't get it done—administratively it wasn't possible. But he persevered for 8 years. We all persevered and just recently I was down there for the opening of this aquaponics unit. It's industry standard: a fishery with all these growing beds for plants. It's run by really sophisticated computer equipment. They have a science teacher who has 16 aquariums there for genetics study. There are going to be effluent growing spots outside the aquaculture unit. The science teacher and kids are going to test how plants grow with and without fertilizer.

When I walked in, I thought, "He and I started talking about this in 1992." When I listened to him talk that night about what his kids had learned and what they can do in that space and then heard him talk to his kids, I thought, "That's why you do all this stuff, because now in this school there is a space where science, math, computer skills, and career skills are going to be taken to the highest level." The unit was filled with people from the community, many of whom had helped to build it. I saw him fully in that context with his students, with their parents, with the real support now of a principal who cared about what he was doing, and with community members who had contributed, and I thought, "This is wonderful." I could tell you a lot of stories like that but that one stands out.

Today, as a writer and advocate for and about the importance of small schools and consequential learning, I can continue my work in an important way, a way in which I hope to reach—and convince—an even broader audience.

SH: Is there anything else you would like to say to our readers?

JS: I would say that it's vital for teachers—and community and other outside support organizations—to collaborate. In the same way that we understood the absolute, essential nature of collaboration between community, schools, and teachers statewide in Alabama, our opportunity to collaborate with Foxfire was part of that whole notion that you just don't get things done in isolation. We had many teachers who profited from being associated with Foxfire, REAL, and other organizations. The strong results that came out of those collaborations reinforced for me the need for people to work together. It's really remarkable. I think about it a lot. Foxfire was like another place I worked. It made for a bigger and richer world. The collaboration was wonderful.

Secondly, I would tell teachers to always remember that they are among a community's most vital resources. I was aware of that very early in life and, partly, I'm prejudiced: My mother was a rural country school teacher. We have a son who teaches in a rural school. I live in my great-grandfather's house and he started a one-room school. So I guess it was in my experience within my family that teaching is an honorable and a good thing and does honor to people. That's in my background and my understanding. I think that teachers and communities must have and support that same understanding.

SH: How did you know to connect with teachers rather than institutions?

JS: It's not easy to know to do that. But if we took a top-down approach, one of two things would happen when we went in to talk to the superintendent or principal and tell them what we had in mind. Either the superintendent is going to say, "Well, that's wonderful," and call the teachers and say, "Do it." The teachers would resent that—at least, I thought they would; and if I were a teacher, I would. Or on the other hand, the superintendent or principal might say, "You can't do that." So there you are up a tree. So we decided we should start with the people who are the most essential—the teachers. First of all, because we knew they were going to do the work, and second, because, often, the teachers were going to invent the work. So it was just logical to start with them. We have never initiated any program in the PACERS Better School Program that was not derived primarily from our collaboration with teachers, students, and community members, but primarily with teachers.

We've always said, "We want the community to be involved, we want students in on the conversation," because we felt that, a lot of the time, teachers are left on their own; and we didn't want that to happen—we wanted to form partnerships; we wanted them to form partnerships.

Chapter Twelve

BOBBY ANN STARNES

Letting Go of the Need to Be Certain, Exploring Possibilities

Bobby Ann Starnes has been a teacher, writer, and educational change proponent for the past 30 years. Her teaching experience ranges from serving as founding director and head teacher of a private school for children from ages 18 months to 12 years to, most recently, teaching sixth grade at Rocky Boy's Indian Reservation in Montana.

After earning a doctorate in Teaching, Curriculum, and Learning Environments at Harvard University, she served as executive director of a large inner-city agency that provided job training, teen-parent, and day care programs for women trying to get off welfare. She was an education department faculty member and chair at a small liberal arts college. She served as president of Foxfire from 1994 through 2000. As Foxfire's second president and through her vision and strong leadership, she brought the organization through a difficult time and re-energized its work to new levels of influence in the field of educational change.

The author of numerous articles for journals, newspapers, and digests, her books include: *From Thinking to Doing* (co-authored by Angela Carone, with Cynthia Paris, 2000), and *About Teachers and Teaching* (co-edited by Maria Broderick, Dan Chazen, Sandra Lawrence, and Paul Naso, 1988); and an issue of *Harvard Educational Review*, Ralph Edwards and Bobby Ann Starnes, Eds. (1988).

Starnes's column, "Thoughts on Teaching," appears regularly in *Phi Delta Kappan*. She lives in Opelika, Alabama, with her cat, Roscoe, and is at work on a book tentatively titled *White Teachers, Indian Children* (Scarecrow Press).

Interview—Summer 2000

SH: At Foxfire, we believe reflecting on memorable learning experiences can inform our own teaching practice. Can you tell us about a memorable learning experience you had?

BAS: One of the things that had an enormous impact on my life happened when in graduate school working with Eleanor Duckworth. She is *the* expert in her field. As we worked together, I was surprised to learn she didn't know everything. It sounds sort of silly now, but it is true. She let us know she wasn't sure about things, she puzzled over things. She would let us see her confusion about a thought, or she would point out that she had been wrong about one thing or another—or that she had revised her thinking as a result of conversations with us teaching fellows or other students. That had a remarkable impact on me. For the first time as a learner, I was able to let go of the need to be certain, the need to *know*, the need to be able to say something without question. Seeing that this woman, this expert, whom I held in such high esteem, was uncertain and that she explored her uncertainties in order to continue to grow and learn, made me free to do the same.

The experience informed all my teaching after that. I wanted anyone I worked with to know that, although I knew some things, I was still struggling to make sense out of it all. So something one of them might say in class or in a conversation would help me to reframe everything I thought I understood. This became a central theme in my teaching, in my life, really. I wanted to help people understand that it's only when we say, "I don't get it," that we can ever come to get it, and that we can never fully get it. We have to shoot for the "it" of the moment. That will lead to the "it" of the next moment, so the "its" are each a step in building more understanding.

SH: Do you remember a significant learning experience you had as a teacher?

BAS: At my school, we had a class for kids between 18 months and 3 years. Nicholas was maybe as old as 2. Now there was no rule in our school that kids had to push the chairs under the tables, but one day Nicholas, for some reason, decided he needed to put the chair under the table. Well, one floor tile was raised a teeny bit, so the bottom of his chair got caught on the tile and wouldn't slide under. So he posed a problem for himself—how could he get the chair under the table? The problem belonged completely to him. He had run into an obstacle and he worked hard to figure it out. He would not give up. I would have. I would have said, "Well, forget it. There's no rule that says it has to be under the table. No one cares if I do this or not." But in fact somebody *did* care—he cared. He struggled for 15 minutes. His teacher and I stood there and watched him as he manipulated the chair this way and that. He was so small, but we could see his wheels turning. Finally, he figured out there was a rise in the tile. He moved the chair over, not by accident, but by trial and error, by remarkable determination, by hard thinking.

Well, this was amazing to me. First of all, he was very young. But more, I was struck by the power that setting his own problem had for him. It was so important that no obstacle could keep him from solving the problem. Now I knew that when people set their own problems and devise ways to solve them using their own creative and innovative solutions, they are more engaged and their attention spans are longer. But here was this sterling example that made me *really* know it. So often that image would come back to me, whether I was teaching kids or adults. The idea that as the teacher, I need to help people pose problems for themselves which they will be driven to answer, to work much harder than I expect them to work, and to care much more deeply about what they're doing. So my challenge became: How do I create an environment where learners can create Nicholas's moment for themselves? How do I create situations where those moments happen not once but over and over again, where learners feel the joy in those moments, and where they learn to create an environment for themselves in which those moments will arise? How can I help learners to reflect on and understand more about those moments—what we at Foxfire call the aesthetic experience, the great joy of learning?

SH: Do you remember mistakes you made as a teacher? Can you give an example of a mistake you made and tell us if and how that experience changed your thinking about teaching?

BAS: A million. One stands out most because it was the most striking wake-up call I can remember ever getting. I was a first-year teacher; in fact, it was my first few weeks of teaching. I had 36 sixth graders. There was a child in my class named Nolan Garber. Nolan dressed and acted in a way I had learned meant kids weren't paying too much attention to life, that they weren't too in tune. So as a first-year teacher, my expectations for him were low because I thought he was a poor student. It's embarrassing, really. I should have known better. I did know better intellectually.

One day I was trying to do a lesson about our little town of Lewisburg, which was founded before Dayton. But while Dayton had become a major industrial center, Lewisburg had remained very small. The answer, of course, was that the Ohio River is by Dayton, and so transportation and businesses grew up around it. But I wanted them to "discover" the answer. I asked all these leading questions, and the kids would answer, "Because all the shopping malls are in Dayton." "Because, a lot of people live there."

It went on this way, and I was so exasperated. Finally, Nolan, sitting in the back of the room, put his hand up. It was as though he was saying to me, "OK. I have seen you struggle enough. I'm amused by your struggles, but it's time for us to move on." He said, so matter-of-factly, "The reason is this: The Miami River flows through Dayton and into the Ohio River, which feeds into the Mississippi, which empties into the Gulf of Mexico. That made trade easy. Here, we don't have a river." Period.

Imagine, I had all these "enlightened" views about class and culture and setting high expectations, and I thought I was so informed. Then, BAM! I realized I had judged that boy and decided he was not very smart be-cause he didn't look like the stereotype I had unknowingly—and to my shame—accepted about what smart kids look like. My personal values crashed down around me as I realized I was a bigot. Then there was my sense of teaching and being an educator, which I was so proud of. I thought, "Well, some kind of educator you are!"

I've probably made that mistake a million times since. No matter how hard we fight against it, it's so hard not to make that mistake—we all have prejudices in us and their ugly heads poke out when we least expect it. This experience made me try not to have the arrogance to think I understand what other people know, what they understand, what meanings they're making—to really fight actively against such thinking, having been taught a lesson very revealingly and powerfully by Nolan Garber. I'll never forget it.

SH: You have a strong sense of the importance of connection to com-munity in learning. How did you come to this understanding?

BAS: When I was 5, my family migrated out of eastern Kentucky where my father was a coal miner. When I went to school, the first thing I learned was that it was not good to be who I was—a hillbilly out of place and out of step with the city culture. My parents were sacrificing greatly to move there because they hated every minute away from our Kentucky home. It wasn't where we belonged. But it was where the opportunities were, and my parents were very big on the importance of education even though they themselves didn't have much. My father was just marginally able to read and my mother only went to sixth grade; but it was the Ameri-can dream to them—for us to get a good education and have opportuni-ties not available to them. My parents thought very little of themselves their whole lives; their dreams were not for themselves but for us.

So they had made a great sacrifice. I knew it, but I also knew I was out of place. What the school told me in very direct ways, really, was that being who I was, being from where I was from, and being the child I was,

was not good. I needed to become Jane in *Dick and Jane*. My house needed neat rows of flowers, my father needed to wear a suit and carry a briefcase, and my mother needed to wear an apron, not work in a fireworks factory.

I got the message. And since it was so important to my parents that we get an education, to have choices they never had—I gave up who I was. So for a long time I would deny I was from eastern Kentucky. And I worked hard to get rid of my accent. Looking back on it, I see the school's message to me was that the more I learned to act like the middle-class White people in our books, the more highly my intellectual skills would be appraised. That's why I should have understood Nolan, and I didn't. That's why it hurt so much and why I jabbed myself so much about it.

In my growing up, all of my education was about changing me and separating me from my culture and from my true community. When I started teaching, I couldn't verbalize what had happened to me. I didn't know it all yet; it unfolded over my adulthood.

But I did know right from the start that kids need to value who they are and where they are from. I didn't want kids to feel they had to deny who they were. I had to help kids celebrate who they were and use that as a foundation for being all that they might become. I knew it from having lived it; the cost is way too high, too high to pay to get moved to the front of the class. And it's not a necessary fee. You don't have to pay. People who sound like I sounded deserve to be in the front of the class. People who look like Nolan deserve to be in the front of the class. So, I wanted kids to know first, be who you are. It enriches all of us. From there you can go where you dream.

SH: In your practice as a teacher, have there been times when you experienced a sense of isolation and lack of support for your work?

BAS: Yes. I taught in the district where I had grown up. I obviously had issues with them. I wanted to teach differently and better and show them it was possible. So I was a radical in terms of celebrating who you are, being connected to the community, and making sure kids got a rigorous education so they could make life choices. Of course I didn't find a school full of like-minded people.

SH: Then how did you overcome the isolation and lack of support?

BAS: I found one person in my school or one person in another school and I connected to that person—we would nourish one another. People didn't have to be exactly like me; we just had to agree on some pretty basic things like kids were good, every kid could learn, the value of democracy, and the value of who people are. Those are not little things. We would vent, we would talk and reflect and puzzle, and then we would figure out what we were going to do.

We not only supported each other by venting and thinking and processing, we focused on taking as much control of our lives as we could. We were proactive. For example, if I found someone I enjoyed teaching with, we would work hard to get our rooms across the hall from each other and to be able to teach the same subject matter, to share some kids and have the kids see both of us as their teachers.

We tried to think about how much the principal could take from us, but not all at once. We would decide, "We won't tell him today that we want to have our kids think of both of us as their teachers, but maybe next fall or spring." It was really about strategizing. We believed we could do more than just talk; we could take action. And we became activists for change. We became active in our local "professional organizations," as we called the NEA in those days. We wanted to be active decision-makers. We got on committees and the principal's council and worked hard to be inside the loop. We knew it mattered because somebody was making decisions that affected our lives and we needed to know who they were and we needed to influence them. We knew we couldn't just close our doors and let some mysterious others make decisions that would control and limit our teaching decisions.

SH: You've been in education a long time. What is it in what you do and how you think about your work that inspires you to continue working?

BAS: It's something new every day. When I taught, no two moments were ever alike, let alone two years. We have this idea that learning is like peeling an onion. But when you peel an onion and get to the center of it, you can say it's all peeled. With teaching you can never do that. People are complex, enormous possibilities always unfolding; and *I* can't do anything to unfold them except create an environment where *they* can unfold themselves. In teaching, I was always trying to understand what would help learners unfold. There's no end to it, and that's a great joy for me. I know that the day I die I will be trying to understand something about how to be a better teacher. I will not be doing what I was doing the day before and I will not be understanding the way I was understanding the day before. How could anyone not be excited by those prospects?

SH: Do you still think of yourself as a teacher?

BAS: I think I teach every day.

SH: How?

BAS: We're not often taught to celebrate the exploration of what we might be; we're taught to be *something*, rather than thinking how wonderful it would be to explore and push ourselves to be what we might be. So every day I try to create an environment where people around me can always learn and always explore a new part of themselves. I try to do that with all parts of my work. When I work with teachers, that's all I'm trying to do. I don't know the potential and possibilities that live in them, but I know there's more than either they or I understand. The challenge is figuring out how we get at that. To me it's the same thing I was doing in the classroom.

SH: Are there things you see in the work of teachers with learners that give you hope for education today?

BAS: Yes. I see an educational environment today that says all that matters is what can be measured by numbers, quantitatively measured, that makes teachers use programs requiring scripts and requiring things teachers don't believe in. In spite of all that, I know that in classrooms around this country there are teachers doing such things because they are required to do it, but at every moment they're widening the crack in the wall, they are not allowing the part of them that brought them to teaching, the part that makes them a good teacher, the part that is their potential, to be smothered. Ultimately, it is their will, their stubbornness, that will take us to a different level, will help us recover from what I believe is a very repressive, counterproductive, and undemocratic teaching and learning environment.

SH: Is there anything you'd like to say to teachers about teaching?

BAS: Remember why you're there. Don't give it up. Celebrate every day the great opportunity you have to make a difference in the lives of children. There's nothing better than teaching. Celebrate it, enjoy it, and take pride in it.

TEACHING AND EDUCATIONAL CHANGE

The three interview subjects in Part V present us with challenging ideas about education, the teaching process, and preconceived methods of gauging learning. Provocative at times, they nevertheless excite discussion and debate.

Chapter Thirteen

ALFIE KOHN

Offering Challenges and Creating Cognitive Dissonance

Alfie Kohn writes and speaks widely on human behavior, education, and social theory. Of his eight books, the best known are: *Punished by Rewards: The Trouble with Gold Stars, Incentive Plans, A's, Praise, and Other Bribes* (1993), *No Contest: The Case Against Competition* (1986), and *The Schools Our Children Deserve: Moving Beyond Traditional Classrooms and "Tougher Standards"* (1999). His most recent book is *The Case Against Standardized Testing: Raising the Scores, Ruining the Schools* (2000). He also has written for the *New York Times*, *Educational Leadership*, *Education Week*, and *Phi Delta Kappan*.

Kohn recently was described by *Time* magazine as "perhaps the country's most outspoken critic of education's fixation on grades [and] test scores." His criticisms of competition and rewards have helped shape the thinking of educators—as well as parents and managers—across the country and abroad.

Kohn lectures widely at universities and to school faculties, parent groups, and corporations. In addition to speaking at staff development seminars and keynoting national education conferences on a regular basis, he conducts workshops for teachers and administrators on various topics. Among them are: "Motivation from the Inside Out: Rethinking Rewards, Assessments, and Learning" and "Beyond Bribes and Threats: Realistic Alternatives to Controlling Students' Behavior." The latter corresponds to his book *Beyond Discipline: From Compliance to Community* (1996), which he describes as "a modest attempt to overthrow the entire field of classroom management."

Kohn lives (actually) in Belmont, Massachusetts, and (virtually) at www.alfiekohn.org.

Interview—Winter 1997

SH: At Foxfire, providing opportunities for students to make their own decisions—student choice—is extremely important in all we do. When did you become aware of the need for student choice, and what are some of the ways you involved students in your classes?

AK: I became aware of most of what students need *after* I taught, I'm sorry to report. I did several things that in retrospect gave me some source of satisfaction or pride, but a lot more that make me wince when I look back on how little I knew about what teachers ought to do. I brought students in for the most part in a peripheral way in deciding how they would respond to an essay question or to pick from a range of questions when it was time for assessment because that was all I knew, it was all that I had experienced from elementary school to graduate school. I missed the point about how important it is for kids to have substantial amounts of discretion in figuring out what they're going to learn and how and why. I came to that belatedly from watching teachers who were much better than I was, reading research and other people's views from Dewey to the present day, and thinking about it a lot. Were I to go back in the classroom today, I would certainly do things differently.

SH: In witnessing other teachers, did you observe obstacles they encountered, and can you tell us how they dealt with them?

AK: One major impediment to giving students choice is the teacher's own reservations about it. Another obstacle is that the students themselves are unaccustomed to freedom and react, at least at first, by engaging in more kinds of behavior, good and bad, than they ever have before because the controls have finally been loosened. They're able to exercise their autonomy for the first time and that's messy and noisy and aggravating. The teachers I've talked to always suggest patience and also bringing the students in on this very problem. Then if, for example, students make ridiculous choices or sit there paralyzed, unable to do anything except to say, "You're the teacher; this is your job," the great teachers are able to react without resentment and too much confusion. They say, "What a great topic for discussion! What's my job? How do you feel when someone tells you what to do all day? Will you say you're too young to make decisions?" Or if students are sitting there impassive during class, that opens all kinds of possibilities, providing the teacher can figure out why this is happening. Is it because they don't feel safe in this classroom? If so, how can *we* change this situation so that nobody is afraid of being left out? If students are sitting there quietly because they have nothing to say at the moment, then forcing them to speak up is worse than doing nothing. If they're merely shy by temperament, that leads you to react in a very different way than if they don't feel their comments are going to be taken seriously.

I think most teachers who have tried to give students choices have realized that the worst of all possible courses is to ask their opinion and then dismiss it—for example, by saying they haven't made a responsible choice, which means they haven't done what the teacher wanted and that, therefore, their decision doesn't count. They feel used and are unlikely to make that mistake again. I always advise teachers to start out with a decision or a question that is circumscribed and the results of which they can live with, until they are able to fashion with the students a classroom that's more democratic.

I made a few efforts along those lines when I was teaching. I gave them the chance to write in journals back before that was fashionable. I'm not sure if it was the dimension of choice to make the decision about what to write or what made that such a good decision. It opened up a new world to me of the students' inner lives. I went from looking at the surface of the ocean to becoming Jacques Cousteau, explorer of the deep, where even students who had never come up to talk to me, and who would not feel safe talking in front of their peers about the things that gripped their inner lives, were opening up to me. If only because it created a kind of relationship under the surface or alongside our public life in the classroom, it was a valuable decision. The only restraint I put on the journals was that they be something more than a dry chronicle of events. They had to talk about how they thought or felt about what was going on and, of course, I promised them confidentiality. That stuff was far richer and more meaningful to them than almost anything I was doing in the regular curriculum.

SH: Did you encounter obstacles?

AK: With the journals, no, primarily not. But I wish I had done more along those lines so that I could have had to work through obstacles I know good teachers do every day. It took me some years to figure this out but . . . either you believe the course is fully formed and delivered to the students or, before the first day of class, you realize that there is nothing but a framework and hunches and first starts and the course itself remains to be created together. I think I see it now but I didn't then. It's not just a matter of how much choice about what books they're going to read; it is a matter of a philosophy of teaching. So a lot of the bumps and barriers and obstacles that great teachers encounter, I, like the great majority of teachers, never had to contend with because I was not teaching authentically to begin with. That's a hard thing for me to admit, and I can only say I wish I had seen it sooner.

SH: Many of our readers tell us they feel isolated in teaching environments that are not supportive. In your own work, have there been times when you felt this isolation and lack of support?

AK: I taught one year at a small independent school in rural Pennsylvania where I was the only person doing even rudimentary progressive things, and I had no support whatsoever for that. This was a girls' school and I was the closest thing to a feminist on campus. I think it was the social and political challenge I posed that isolated me more than my pedagogical practice, in part because of how reactionary and cloistered a community it was.

SH: How did you get through that?

AK: By keeping my own journal and talking to myself because there was no one to talk to. I wrote letters to my friends and read voraciously, but my frustration was poured out into the pages of what turned out to be a book-length manuscript about what I was facing. I draw material from that year that has informed my thinking ever since. I'll give you one example which I have thought about often. I had one class that year where the kids gave me a terrible time. They, as I see it, must have stayed up nights trying to figure out how to make my life a living hell because they couldn't have been that good at it spontaneously. I'm able to laugh about it now but I was reduced almost to tears sometimes because of the solid wall of hostility I met in that classroom. I thought I was doing things right; you know, I didn't just give them Wordsworth to read, I would give them Joni Mitchell, but I might as well have given them Hegel in the original German. At one point, I said, "Fine, you find me the song lyrics and you can teach them."

But that didn't change the atmosphere in the classroom—it came no closer to creating a situation where we were on a mission of learning together. If you had asked me then what I needed, I would have replied in an instant that I needed a classroom management system, a way to discipline these kids who were obstreperous and noncompliant. What I realize now is I really needed a curriculum worth learning. For the most part, I was using *Warriner's,* which is essentially "Our Friend, the Adverb" stuff that few members of our species would find intrinsically motivating. And I resorted, to my later shame, to the grade book, that combination of bribes and threats, to make them learn this material. What I realized much later was that I needed for them to have more choices; I needed a more accurate view of how learning happens and the respects in which students have to construct meaning for themselves instead of swallowing whole the ideas and skills offered to them by a teacher. So that one experience has colored my view of classroom management and the respects in which it is inextricable from, and largely a function of, the academic learning that's going on in a classroom.

SH: Many teachers struggle with how to help students learn to make good choices. Have you struggled with that, and what is your thinking on it?

AK: Well, the first step in making a good choice is to *have* a choice rather than being told what to do most of the time. Kids learn to make good decisions by making decisions, not by following directions. If we want our kids to take responsibility for their behavior, then we have to *give* them responsibilities—along with guidance and support and love. But they also have to be making decisions that matter. I often hear teachers talk about how they give kids the chance to choose, when the teachers don't really care about the outcome and, of course, that's nothing close to a democratic classroom. The kids have to be able to make decisions when it matters very much to the teacher because that's authentic choice. We help kids make good choices by making sure they are informed about the options they have and also that the options are appealing. A kid who gets to choose between two workbooks or silly essay questions or the time of day in which to memorize math facts is not being offered real choice. Somewhere Shakespeare says there is little choice in rotten apples.

SH: Have you talked to teachers who are struggling with this, and do you see them finding positive solutions?

AK: Yes, absolutely. That's where I've learned most of what's going on in my thinking. It's the practical realities in classrooms around the country I've witnessed that animate my work and inform it. When I walk into a second-grade classroom in St. Louis and watch the kids running their own class meetings to solve problems that have come up, where one child is the facilitator and another is the recorder—thus teaching language skills—and the teacher is just sprawled out on the floor with the rest of them as they maintain a discipline, a patience, and a respect that would have blown me away if they were 17, but they were in fact 7 years old. Or the story of a teacher in California who came back from her break to find the kids already huddled together excitedly talking about something even though recess wasn't over, and when she asked what was going on, was told a problem had happened during recess and they were holding a meeting to fix it by themselves. The kids didn't get there right away. In both those examples—and many others I could share—what I'm really looking at is the hard work of the teacher in helping them to become empowered, to take responsibility not only for their own behavior but for the actions and values and feelings of everyone else, as well as learning the skills of how to make decisions together.

For heaven's sake, most books and classes to which teachers are exposed take it for granted that the teacher must be in control of the classroom and the only question is how you get and keep that control most effectively. What I want to call into question is the idea that the teacher ought to be in unilateral control of what's going on. I didn't question that premise when I was teaching. I never saw a classroom where a group of learners democratically figured out what the course ought to be, what to learn, how to learn, why to learn, how to treat each other, how they wanted to solve problems. I'd never read about or seen it, so my classrooms reflected my own experience. I imagine that's true for millions of teachers around the country. It's all the more remarkable, then, when you come across an example of somebody who miraculously has figured out that kids have to be active learners and that the best teaching is not where the teacher is most firmly in charge.

SH: Looking at the concept of awards, when you were teaching were you deeply entrenched in the concept of awards? How did you move away from giving awards, and what obstacles did you encounter?

AK: One of the few things I figured out on my own was that I had to do everything possible to neutralize the destructive effects of these things [grades] that I was required to give.

I taught for a while at a school of kids who had been prepared to get into Harvard since their earliest days, a process I have come to call Preparation H, and these were kids for whom the absence of grades creates what I can only call existential vertigo. I told the kids that I had to give them grades at the end although I didn't like it, and then I told them why I didn't like it.

Today what I hope I would do is bring them in on a discussion of the effects of grades and invite them to reflect on how it has led them to do only what is required and to pick the easiest possible assignments so as to maximize the probability of getting an A, and so on.

What I've since learned is that the best teachers do a lot more asking than telling. But at least I figured out that the grades themselves were destructive and I said to them, "I have to give you a grade at the end of the term, but I cannot in good conscience ever put a letter or a number on anything you do, and I won't. All I will do when time permits is write a comment and/or talk to you about what you've done."

Now that could have backfired easily if I'd left it at that because some of them would have been led to think even more about their grades: Now I was keeping their grades a secret from them, and that would have been counterproductive in the extreme. So I told them that if they really needed to know what grade this paper would get or what grade they would get if one were given at this point in the term, they could come up and see me and we would talk together.

I'm pleased to report that as time went on, fewer students felt the need to do that because when I stopped pushing these grades into their faces by writing one on a paper they had written for me, they began to be more engaged with the subject matter. At some point I had to give them a grade, but I wasn't going to make it any more salient than I had to; and that's a piece of advice I give to teachers now. Until we're able to work together to eliminate traditional letter grades, which I believe are inimical to real learning, we need to do everything we can in our own classrooms to make them invisible.

SH: Is there anything you would like to say to our teacher-readers about the work of teaching?

AK: When I conclude one of my own presentations, I try to leave teachers with two points. One is that if they have heard me say something that struck a nerve and made them extremely uncomfortable because I have indicted a practice they just engaged in that very morning, they might be tempted to wonder whether they are bad teachers. In fact, if they are even thinking in those terms, they are probably terrific teachers because they have the courage to be open to the possibility that they have done something not as well as it could have been done. The people who look stricken and gulp are the people whose classroom I want my kid in because they have the gumption to try to get better at what they do.

The other thought I might close with is that if someone is inclined to take a chance and do something different—not just adding some new technique like getting kids on the internet, but really rethinking the whole philosophy of learning—they shouldn't try to do it alone. They should, at the very least, find a colleague to provide moral support and new ideas to help them avoid being burned out and depressed. For those who are bringing kids in on making decisions only to have the kids the very next year go back to workbooks and assertive discipline, it can be demoralizing. I always ask those teachers if there was a teacher when *they* were kids who made a difference in their lives in just one year. I tell them they can be that teacher. But they can't be that teacher over time unless they have found somebody to complain to and be inspired by. You know, we are interdependent creatures, like it or not. I think we might as well like it, own it, and recognize that we can both provide support and derive support from others, even in an environment that isn't as welcoming as it ought to be.

IRA SHOR

Teaching and Cultural Democracy

Ira Shor grew up in the Jewish working-class South Bronx, New York City.
He was a boy scientist with a chemistry
set who loved to read and who dreamed
of becoming a rich doctor when he
grew up. Life delivered other plans,
and he became a teacher, writer, and
activist instead.

Shor is Professor of English at the
City University of New York Graduate
School and at the College of Staten Is-
land. For 2000–2001, he was on leave
from CUNY to serve as Distinguished
Visiting Professor at William Paterson University in New Jersey where he
taught courses in whiteness studies and in patriarchy. He received his Ph.D.
from the University of Wisconsin in 1971.

His latest books include a tribute to his friend and mentor, *Paulo Freire:
Critical Literacy in Action* and *Education in Politics*, Vols. I and II (1999–2000).
Other recent books include: *When Students Have Power* and *Empowering
Education*. Currently, he is researching a new book on social class in school
and society.

A member of the Green Party, Shor is an avid sports fan and a swing
dancer.

Interview—Summer 1998

SH: At Foxfire we believe reflecting on another's learning experiences
can inform our own teaching practice. Can you tell us about one of your
memorable learning experiences?

IS: Yes. I was the kind of student who loved reading, learning, and books, but hated school. You know, kids are very curious beings. We like learning things—tell me, show me, explain why. But school was boring and insulting. It taught me a lesson about the difference between learning and schooling—that formal education is one thing and human curiosity, human desire for knowledge, is another. I sat in school for 12 years swallowing information without inspiration, while outside school, I had a million questions about life and the world.

SH: How do those experiences inform your work today?

IS: I've had to ask myself, how come school produces boredom and anti-intellectualism, how does schooling produce people who don't like to read, write, or study? I want to prevent my own classes from being as boring and insulting as I remember most of my schooling. As a teacher, I want to appeal to the students' desire to learn and to their innate curiosity. I want my classroom environment to be challenging and questioning and interactive and participatory and stimulating and, in a sense, maybe unsettling, to challenge students to rethink things.

I believe students should be treated as complicated, substantial human beings who have a right to take part in the making of their own education. Education should not be done to them, but education should be something they do with each other for themselves. We have to overcome the passivity that makes intellectual life, mental life, so repulsive to many students.

I have asked myself—what can I do as a teacher so that people love learning, love writing, love challenges, [and] see intellectual life as an essential part of their experience?

SH: Did you experience times when you felt frustrated and overwhelmed by the challenges you faced as a teacher?

IS: Yes. For the past 30 years, the City University of New York, where I teach, has been under conservative attack. In the 1970s our historic open admissions program was denounced as a welfare boondoggle throwing good money away on people who didn't deserve higher education. There was a very powerful campaign in the mass media and among authorities to demonize the nonelite student. So every year we fight prodigious battles to defend ourselves, prove our worth, and mobilize students to protect the university. It's been a difficult time to be in the public sector and for cultural democracy.

SH: What motivated you and helped you through those difficult times?

IS: I believed in what I'm doing. I believe education should serve equality and that our task is to build a multicultural democracy in the United States. The great opportunity in New York in 1971 to develop cultural democracy with open admissions inspired me as a young teacher. I was very hopeful that we could pioneer a new road to learning in society. Also, I had colleagues who were inspired and that helped. And, at that time because of the activist 1960s, students were still optimistic and felt they could accomplish something meaningful in society by working together for change. I also started writing a lot in the 1970s and the writing helped me through the worst of times. I was able to put my education experiences on paper and publish them to make sense out of the critical teaching I was doing. Then I came across Paulo Freire's work in the 1970s and his books were very inspiring. I met Freire himself in the early 1980s and we spent a bunch of years working together, so that also helped me to deal with the difficulties.

SH: He must have been a very inspiring person.

IS: Yes, Paulo Freire was one of a kind. There's no one who can take his place. His sudden death in May 1997 really hurt. I miss him a lot. Around Paulo, you felt like eating, dancing, falling in love, and changing the world.

SH: In your writing you address sharing power in the classroom. As a teacher trying to empower students, were there times when you felt a sense of isolation and lack of support from other teachers and administrators?

IS: Yes. This is common for teachers who innovate student-centered methods. Formal education, the school system from kindergarten to graduate school, is restrictive and institutional. It's set up bureaucratically by authority and controlled from the top down. So all of us who believe in democratic education—that is, education from the bottom up, student-centered education, power sharing, and developing critical thought against the unequal status quo—we have to teach against the system, against the institution, which represents the existing authority, the inequalities that we're born into.

SH: Do you have advice for other teachers who are in similar situations trying to empower students?

IS: Yes, I think it is important to find allies among other teachers and work with them so that you avoid isolation. Paulo Freire used to say that we can't confront the lion alone. For him, the power of the status quo is like a lion, and the only way to confront the lion is in organized groups. So we must find allies. With these allies we must experiment, innovate, start small study groups of teachers to read books, and also examine the work we do in the classroom. I would also think it important to include students as allies in the experiments that we undertake in the classroom. Wherever possible, we need to meet with parents to discuss what we are doing and to include the parents, consult with them so they feel they're partners in the students' education.

I'd encourage teachers to write as much as possible about the classes they teach because writing is very educational. We need to keep journals and send our writings to other teachers for response. This would be a very good way to network and to clarify what we're trying to do. Paulo thought it very important for teachers to organize their own development and to join in larger coalitions for social change.

Also, I would invite teachers to get involved in their teacher unions. We have to push together in a progressive direction for smaller class size, for reduced course loads, for improved working conditions, for more authority, for equal funding. We have to make sure schools offer good facilities and up-to-date books, computers, and rich cultural programs to all students, not only those in wealthy districts. We have to organize to see that the great wealth of our society is invested equally in all children. We have to be very clear about how to function politically to support public education against privatization schemes, against voucher schemes, against "defunding" and budget cuts, against the imposition of more standardized testing, against required syllabi written by a committee a hundred miles away. Without strong, progressive unions, I don't see how we're going to get those things. As I see it now, teachers are heavily unionized but the teacher unions are not activist promoters of democracy and equality. The current leadership is part of the status quo, not critical of it.

SH: In implementing student empowerment in your classrooms, what were some of the obstacles you encountered from students?

IS: I have to overcome student disregard and suspicion of new ways of working together. Students come through mass education that is teacher-centered, test-oriented, and textbook-dominated, so they grow up in the passive, direct-instruction model, which teaches them that education means listening to a teacher or reading a textbook. They're not invited to see education as their active responsibility to make meaning, to examine things, and to use knowledge to change their conditions. So, when I present them with a problem-posing class in a dialogic format, there's doubt and skepticism. They have not had a chance to develop their democratic talents and habits, which dialogue education needs. There's also immaturity because some students are young and don't know how to behave in a classroom that doesn't have traditional discipline or a traditional grading system. Also, a lot of students have been bored for so long in school that it's hard for them to notice something different is going on, because school has been so remote and alien to the language they use, to their interests. For many students, school has been dull and insulting—about someone else's world, not theirs.

SH: How do you overcome those obstacles?

IS: Every class is like starting over. Every class is a new group of students who arrive socialized into passive education and top-down authority—what Paulo Freire called the banking model—so I have to start over again. I try to make the classroom exciting, intense, inspiring. I also try to pose meaningful problems in language they understand that invite them to work on things, to make the classroom very active so that they don't get the message, "Sit back and listen," but rather, "Sit up and do something together." I use a lot of collaborative learning. We study uses of language a lot. I ask them to construct parts of the syllabus by bringing in readings, by deciding what questions they want to pose for writing and for discussion. These are some methods I use to invite them to be active learners. I pose problems, ask them to pose questions, ask them to bring in readings, ask them to write a lot. They're invited to read their writing and then develop a dialogue in class from their own questions and their own writings. The student-based approach uses their expression as the foundation of the dialogue. I call it front-loading student expression and back-loading teacher interventions.

SH: Was there a deciding moment when you knew you wanted to be a teacher?

IS: Well, the truth is I started out to be a doctor, an M.D. I love science, but I love history, paleontology, and archaeology, too. When young, I loved reading—I was a very bookish kid. My father was a high school dropout who was a sheet-metal worker, and my mother was a bookkeeper who never went to college so I really have no college in the family. We were always short on money—I wore hand-me-downs, and so on. As a kid I figured, "Look, I like to read so maybe I'll stay in school and maybe I'll get rich from my brains. So how do you get rich using your head?" It seemed the richest person in the neighborhood was the doctor, who lived in the suburbs, so I figured I'd be a doctor, and all my relatives wanted me to be a doctor. "Why not me?" I went to the Bronx High School of Science and then to college, where I spent the first 2 years in pre-med. But science was extremely boring to me and I couldn't stand it. It was constant memorization of formulas and equations and periodic tables. It seemed completely uninspiring and out of touch with reality. I was drastically losing interest so I started switching to other disciplines and finally became a literary major. I figured I would write books and literary criticism, poetry, and novels. Then my very first job after my Ph.D. was teaching remedial writing in an open-admissions community college, and I got very inspired by the struggle for cultural democracy. I switched from literature to literacy and from literary scholarship to pedagogy and policy. That's what really made me into a teacher—this moment in history when there was a chance to develop a new pedagogy and take part in cultural democracy.

SH: What advice would you give a teacher who is already in a traditional school system and determines that he or she wants to use innovative methods?

IS: I think that's a very important decision to make, and I hope more teachers do that. If we are veteran teachers in a school that is not changing, then we have to be very good politicians at that school to find allies among parents and students and fellow teachers who will join us at some level of innovation. If we can't find allies, we have to go to professional organizations, attend meetings where we can get support from teachers elsewhere who are experimenting so we don't feel isolated. Or find teachers from other nearby schools if we don't get enough support in our own school. We should be reading journals so we learn from the experience of other teachers. Also get involved in networks like the National Coalition of Education Activists or more involved in Foxfire to find help so that you don't get isolated. Isolation invites us to get discouraged, so we have to find allies. Follow the debate on high-stakes testing, on vouchers, privatization, etc., so you keep up with the issues. Set an example for good teaching so you get known as someone who really works hard for students. That gives you credibility to criticize the status quo.

SH: Is there anything else you would like to say about teaching?

IS: Educators are absolutely essential to society fulfilling its democratic ideals. A democratic society requires democratic schools that develop students as critical and activist citizens. We play an extremely crucial role because the entire population passes through our classrooms. So we have a wonderful opportunity to influence the development of each generation that will influence the development of society. Hopefully, we will take a very strong democratic stance and encourage our colleagues and students to reject racism and sexism and homophobia and the increasing corporate control of the economy. I think those are the issues we have to face. Our jobs as educators are absolutely crucial; but to do it well, we have to think of ourselves as citizen professionals. To me that means being democratic educators who teach for critical thinking, citizen rights, social justice, and equality. And we will be doing this at a time when power and wealth are being concentrated into fewer and fewer private hands. The situation in America is very grave right now in terms of what will happen to our democracy, when power and wealth are being taken away from us and put into the private sector. There has been no more urgent time than now for us to take seriously our role as democratic educators.

Chapter Fifteen

TED SIZER

Extreme Experiences and Asking the Unaskable

Theodore R. Sizer is founder and chairman of the Coalition of Essential Schools, a national network of schools and centers engaged in restructuring and redesigning schools to promote better student learning and achievement.

He is Professor Emeritus at Brown University, where he served as chair of the Education Department from 1984 to 1989. Before coming to Brown, Sizer was professor and dean at the Harvard Graduate School of Education (1964–1972) and headmaster of Phillips (Andover) Academy (1972–1981).

Three of his books, *Horace's Compromise* (1985), *Horace's School* (1992), and *Horace's Hope* (1996), published by Houghton Mifflin, explore the motivation and the ideas of the Essential School reform effort.

In 1999 Sizer joined his wife, Nancy Faust Sizer, as acting principal of the Francis W. Parker Charter Essential School in Devens, Massachusetts, where he serves as a trustee. He and his wife are co-authors of the recently published book *The Students Are Watching: Schools and the Moral Contract* (Beacon Press).

Sizer and his wife live in Harvard, Massachusetts. They have four children, three children-in-law, and nine grandchildren.

[*Editor's Note*: As noted earlier, Elaine Minton, who briefly served as editor of *The Active Learner: A Foxfire Journal for Teachers* in early 1996, conducted this interview.]

Interview—Summer 1996

EM: You probably know that at Foxfire we have a lot of respect for teachers' memorable learning experiences and the ways that thinking about them can inform our own teaching practice. Can you tell us about one of your memorable learning experiences?

TS: Oh, so many rush to mind. In 1958, I went to Australia with my wife and little child and taught for a year in a big Church of England boys' school. The school was organized and run in ways which were quite unfamiliar to me, both from my previous teaching in the States and from my teacher training.

It was quite regimented, and it placed an enormous responsibility on the students to govern themselves. The culture of the school was shaped by the Prefects, the senior boys. The students took seven, eight, or nine subjects at once.

The abler the student, the longer the student stayed in school. The abler student stayed for 3 twelfth-grade years, getting deeper and deeper into various academic subjects. These are examples of all sorts of things which didn't seem to make sense to me.

EM: What are the ways that the lessons you take from it inform your own work?

TS: What I learned there was that context is everything. In most ways, that Australian school was successful for the youngsters there, in a way that it wouldn't have been successful in the northeastern United States. The memorable learning was that you have to be very, very respectful and very sensitive to the values, to the attitudes, that the youngsters bring into class, that their parents have, which the community has. Ever since then, I've been loathe to say there's "one best way" to do anything, because culture and context count so much.

EM: Was there a moment when you knew that you were a teacher?

TS: I don't think there was a moment, but if there was one, it probably was during my years in the army. I went into the army right after graduating from college. I was put into a teaching role . . . the troops for which I was responsible played out what I presumably taught them. But, again, I was only 21. I didn't have the readiness to reflect on what I was doing that I now have. Looking back on it, though, they must have had an unsensed impact, as I knew by the time I left the active military that I wanted to be a teacher.

EM: So, do you feel that what you learned in the army had an effect on the work that you've done ever since?

TS: Oh, absolutely. In the army, nobody ever said to me that some soldiers could learn and some other soldiers couldn't learn. Every soldier had to perform. . . . I was responsible for the training and operations of the artillery battery, which was dangerous work. No soldier could be given the opportunity to get a "failing grade" or even to get a C+. Everyone had to perform for safety's sake if for no other. Most of the troops in my original unit were high school dropouts. Many of them did not have English as a home language. All of them performed ultimately very well. They had to. So this now-fancy slogan, "All children can learn," was something I grew up with. People will rise to challenges in spite of our labeling them as "dropouts" and non-English speakers, low testers, all of those things. Get the incentives right, get the teaching right, and almost anybody can learn anything.

EM: Many teachers who read our journal may at times feel overwhelmed and frustrated by the challenges they face. Were there times in your own teaching or schoolwork that you had those feelings?

TS: Going back to my early days in Australia, I taught 180 students; I didn't even know a third of them halfway through the year. I was teaching formulas to kids I didn't know well, and it's from that extreme experience that I learned that unless you know a child well, you can't teach that child very well. And, the heroic loads carried by many secondary school teachers in this country, as well as for me in those days in Australia, simply means that we get to know but a few of the kids well and thereby teach them well. The rest of the youngsters remain sort of foggy in our understanding. That's why, in my current high school work, I feel so strongly about getting the numbers-per-teacher down so that each child has the privilege of being known well by his or her teacher.

EM: What are the things, emotionally, that motivated you and pulled you through these difficult times?

TS: The irrepressible optimism of teenagers. Even in an overheated, crowded room, late in the year, with half a class which has flunked a test, there's always some kid who has a throwaway remark which cracks everybody up. Adolescents, most of them, I think, have a wonderful naiveté that all the problems of the world out there . . . they believe that, individually, each [adolescent] is going to overcome them [the problems]. You and I know they won't, but there is a kind of energy that arises from their inexperience, which ironically, is infectious. There are plenty of kids who don't express it, but there isn't this sort of hangdog quality that you find among many adult groups where nobody thinks they can do anything, where too few people are prepared to do the hard work because they assume that it's impossible.

EM: Many of our readers are teachers who talk about experiencing a sense of isolation and lack of support for the learner-centered, active classrooms they struggle to create. In your own teaching or schoolwork, have there been times when you experienced that sense of isolation and lack of support for your work?

TS: Oh yes. At Brown, I never taught alone. Isolation is bad for everybody, including the students. If I'm the only one teaching a seminar or class, I am the only judge of the student. It depends entirely on me to figure that kid out. And I've learned that if you teach with somebody else, you have another set of eyes. And I might say, "Well, Martha really just can't deal with abstractions." My colleague, who may teach a different subject and see Martha in a different light, will say, "Well, wait a minute; in mathematics, she deals with abstractions in this way. It's just in your history class that different kinds of abstractions are giving her a problem." We do better by the kids when we work collectively. I see this most poignantly among elementary school teachers who, in fact, are running one-room schoolhouses. They don't have any, or very little, adult conversation built into their day, and rarely are there other adults who know their kids, their particular youngsters, very well. So, it's lonely work for the teachers, and it's also not good for the kids.

EM: Is there some practical advice that you could give to those teachers out there who are in that situation? Are there some helpful hints, maybe?

TS: Let's say that I'm a fifth-grade teacher in a self-contained classroom, and I have 30 kids. I go to the principal with my friend in the next room who also teaches fifth grade, and say, "The two of us will take 60 kids, and we will plan together. Give us a room with a folding door; we'll work together on the overall program." Or at the high school level, I'm a math teacher, and I will cluster some of my students with their work, let's say, in AP physics. The AP physics kids will also be taking my calculus course, and the physics teachers whose students are using the calculus and I will constantly be on top of our common kids. We'll really understand them. So, it's a matter of finding your friends and getting the school to let you work with your friends so that you have collegial support.

EM: Are there things you have seen that encourage you or give you hope about the ways teachers are doing their work with learners?

TS: Well, I think that there's a paradox. The condition in many schools, alas, is getting more desperate because of the combination of shrinking real dollars in support of those schools and the often-mindless imposition of rapidly changing mandates and regulations. The paradox resides in the fact that the situation is so bad in many communities that people are prepared to ask questions that they didn't dare ask before. Folks are scared.

EM: What kinds of questions?

TS: High schools with substantial dropout rates, high schools that require tough assistant principals to sweep the halls. At some point people are going to say that maybe we ought to simplify the schools, we ought to break them into smaller schools, we ought to focus on the culture of the school. Which is to say, the situation is so bad that people are beginning to ask questions that they didn't dare to ask before. And, it's the beginning of that "question asking" that leads to a serious improvement in schools.

EM: Of all that you have done in your career, what are the things that have given you the greatest sense of pride or satisfaction?

TS: Oh, that's such a hard question. You have these wonderful moments where the satisfaction is immediate. Some kid that everyone else thought was such a no-hoper crashes through with a terrific performance. Or there's a crisis in the school where you're the principal and somehow the school instantly comes together around that crisis in a wonderful way which not only addresses the critical issue but also teaches a powerful collective lesson. But those are immediate things; longer-range ones are the adults who walk back in your life and say, "Thanks a lot," or "Mr. Sizer, you may not remember but . . . ," and then describe some incident which I had forgotten which somehow had considerable meaning for them, then and now. And, one of the enormous joys of teaching is that you constantly continue being paid back. . . .

EM: Can you give me an example of when that's happened in your life?

TS: Well, one that goes way back. There was a brilliant young man at that school in Australia who was in his third year as a Sixth Former in twelfth grade. He ended up with 15 first-class honors. One year he did all the sciences and math, another year he did all the languages, and the third year he did all his histories. He was an extraordinary kid, but when he went off to the nearest university in Melbourne, he had all sorts of trouble. He could not sustain the academic "hothouse." I lost track of him and eventually heard of his trouble. He had dropped out of the university. Well, about 18 years later, I was in a seminar in England, and I got a phone call at the conference center from this same young Australian—now a Church of England priest in a parish in rural Oxfordshire. Well, sitting down with Peter after all those years and going through his life that followed in his academic hothouse years, meant enough to him to get in touch when he read in the paper that a group of us were meeting nearby. It was very warming. Again, teachers know not often what they do.

My dad was a history of art teacher at Yale from 1927 to 1957. When he died, my mother got a thousand letters from his former students. I learned then to write my respected teachers while they are still alive. . . . How my father would have enjoyed those letters!

EM: Do you think he had a major influence on your wanting to be a teacher?

TS: Oh sure. His combination of rigor and subjectivity has influenced a lot of the way I think about learning. There's a very powerful discipline required in the arts, even as it is "nonmechanical" . . . a mixture of the philosophical and the disciplined.

EM: Did he live long enough to be able to see you become a teacher?

TS: Yes. He died in 1967, and so I had been at the game for some time. Our connections were never more powerful than when he was in his later years.

EM: Are there other things you would like to say to our teacher-readers about the work of teaching?

TS: Most of a teacher's real "victories" are large victories, which you believe at the time to be small victories. And on another theme, we must remember that much of life is a dart board—to give an example, I mean the opportunity while I was still a high school principal at Phillips Academy to start my research on high schools. That unusual opportunity was at the urging of a couple of the school's trustees. They gave encouragement. Foundations came in behind and supported the work. At the end of the research, a few of the foundation leaders said, "Putting books on the shelf is just the beginning. Now what are you going to do with those ideas?" Again, it was because of a few people who said, "Come on, you can't stop what you're doing, keep going." This sort of encouragement can emerge almost serendipitously.

EM: In that vein, what kinds of words of encouragement and hope can you offer to our readers out there who are teaching now?

TS: Always wear bifocal glasses. I mean, look through the bottom half at your own kids and your own colleagues and the culture of your own school. But don't only do that; look up and see how those kids in that school fit into the larger scheme of things. So much of what we do in high schools makes no sense at all; we do it just because we've always done it. And many of us, good folk, trudge on because we're always only looking down through the bottom part of the glasses at the kids we have gathered around us. That's not enough. The way to get the changes, which in many places are badly needed, is for people who know what they're doing to take the time to look up and insist that the changes be made. Those that do look up, while at the same time doing well by their own kids, are the ones who are really going to make a difference.

EM: Do you have anything else that you would like to tell our teachers about teaching?

TS: I would like to say don't keep good student work under a bushel basket. Videotape it, write about it, and share it. Link arms with people who will do the same, who are prepared to show their communities exemplary work from their students. The greatest strength in American education is its army of inspired teachers. They are currently less than the sum of their parts because they haven't linked arms. They operate too much in isolation. What we need are networks, such as Foxfire and the Coalition of Essential Schools or others, that make sure the good work is magnified beyond your or my classroom.

EM: So, you feel encouraged by what you're seeing with the way that things are going and the directions these organizations are taking?

TS: Yes. It's so bleak, it's hopeful. People are asking the unaskable. People are saying the unsayable. That's progress.

Part VI

REFLECTIONS ON POWERFUL CONVERSATIONS

In the final chapter, Sara Hatton weaves connections and comparisons among the ideas, methods, and thinking revealed by the educators presented in the book, and reflects on the great value of continuously seeking something none of us will ever "catch."

Chapter Sixteen

Pursuing Something They Haven't Caught Yet

The sometimes poignant and revealing, often surprising stories shared in the interviews of this book provide a very human picture of these influential educators. Although considered by many to be experts in one way or another, they remain embroiled in the struggle to make meaning. It seems apparent from their interviews that each would agree with Maxine Greene's words, "I'm pursuing something I haven't caught yet." And obviously each takes joy in the pursuit. Still seeking, they fully expect that the answers they know today will move them to higher levels of understanding tomorrow.

How They Work

These extraordinary people go about their work in many ways. Their educational visions seem to be constructed upon similar beliefs; however, the methods and emphasis of their work appear strikingly different. Some, like Sizer and Shelton, take on the task of changing the way schooling occurs by changing the ways schools operate.

Jack Shelton promotes the concept—now validated through research—that meaningful, lasting learning takes place in small settings where students have responsibility for their own learning. Through his guidance of PACERS, which he founded at the University of Alabama over 30 years ago, he supports teachers, schools, and communities in the collaborative creation of hands-on learning laboratories where students engage in curriculum-based work that is meaningful to them and their communities.

Through the Coalition of Essential Schools, Ted Sizer focuses on the creation of schools across the country that are governed by a set of principles through which teaching and learning are equitable, personalized, and intellectually vibrant.

Others, like Greene, Shor, and Noddings, seek to impact schools through philosophical arguments. For example, through her writings and lectures, Greene has brought educators to a new vision of knowing that includes perception, cognition, affect, and the imagination.

Ira Shor addresses the moral imperative to develop cultural democracy through the classroom. He stresses the need for teachers to become "activist promoters of democracy and equality" in education.

Through her writings, Nel Noddings focuses on the ethics of caring, a relational ethic that "emphasizes our moral interdependence" and that promotes the building of inclusive communities.

The arguments put forth by Noddings, Shor, and Greene often support and explain the reasoning underlying the approaches others utilize in their efforts toward school change.

Still others among those interviewed focus their work on what they see as specific problematic causes for failure in education. Alfie Kohn, for example, sees grades and other forms of coercion, as well as standardized tests, as roadblocks to intellectual growth—and to inspired teaching.

Robert Coles, whose self-description varies from researcher, psychiatrist, doctor, educator, writer, storyteller, and more, has built his life's work around looking deeply into the lives of children through observation and interviews. His findings on the moral and spiritual sensibilities of children of cultural, ethnic, and racial minorities give practical application to the theories that drive Sizer, Greene, Shelton, and Kohn.

Others interviewed strive to create viable, vibrant learning environments by concentrating on significant aspects of the educational experience of students.

Yetta Goodman's call to teachers to closely observe children (she coined the word "kid-watching") and her leadership in literacy development have proved a powerful influence on the way teachers think about and teach language in their classrooms.

During the 1970s and 1980s, Donald Graves conducted groundbreaking research into the ways children write. He later published his findings and theories in a series of books on writing development in children across the learning spectrum. These influenced the way writing is taught across the country and around the world.

Vivian Paley provides concrete ways to observe, study, and document the ways children interact in the classroom, and has brought us new insight into a very complex social system.

Through her work as a teacher-educator and writer, Eleanor Duckworth stresses the importance of the experiences and insights of students and places emphasis on understanding how they make sense of the world around them.

Grant Wiggins looks at the use of assessment to understand what learners know. Through his work, he has helped change both the tools that teachers use in the assessment process and the way that they *think* about the process.

The work of Goodman, Graves, Paley, Duckworth, and Wiggins informs teacher practice and provides insights that allow teachers to gain access to important understandings about what is learned and how meaning is made. Like others mentioned here, these educators share certain common beliefs that inform and guide the insightful choices they make about how they will support teaching and learning.

Bobby Ann Starnes and Parker Palmer also center their efforts on teachers, but in different ways. As former president of Foxfire, an organization described as "of, by, and for teachers," Starnes sought to assist teachers in implementing a set of practices that create learner-centered and community-focused classrooms. In her work today as a writer and author, she continues to center her attention on issues of concern to teachers and to advocate for them. In turn, Palmer works to support teachers in their own personal growth toward self-realization, a process he says is necessary before someone can be a true teacher. He exhorts teachers to look within to find ways to teach that are personally meaningful to them.

Taking Meaning from the Interviews

Given the high standing that the interview subjects have in education, readers may have hoped to find conclusive answers to questions that have plagued their thinking or practice for some time. However, these educators make it clear that there is no *one* answer for the questions that bewilder teachers in their daily practice. In fact, they reveal that there isn't a single answer for the questions that perplex and confound the broader issues of educational change. There is no one understanding or vision, no quick answer for problems, and no simple solution or how-to approach to every teaching/learning situation. The problems are too multifaceted and are too couched in specific circumstances. The solutions are complicated and must be addressed within environments that have their own dynamics, cultures, and standards of behavior.

Instead of finding answers or solutions, these interviews raise more questions. Although some practical applications can be identified in the interviews, what emerges most powerfully is a series of similar, yet unique, intellectual frameworks that form the basis of the understanding, method, and emphasis each of these educators has chosen.

Analysis of the interviews, therefore, allows each reader to make his or her own interpretation of the meaning and importance of the interviews. As Eleanor Duckworth points out, each will have her or his "own ways of making sense." Therefore, each will find lessons and insights most appropriate to individual teaching situations, struggles, and practice. In addition, readers will find new messages, lessons, and inspirations with each reading.

At the same time, reading the interviews reveals themes among the distinct voices and personalities. These include: being a work in progress, the nature of teaching, optimism for the future, the role of the teacher, teachers as activists, the essential nature of mistakes, the value of reflection, learning from kids, what's important to teach, allies, the value in community, the role of mentors, on being different, and connecting experience and practice. These themes are relevant to anyone interested in, or already practicing, teaching.

In addition, they create a certain organization of thought that allows readers to zero in on those ideas that are personally meaningful and resonant, as well as digest what is new and foreign. Those just beginning to explore approaches to teaching and learning may find these themes helpful in organizing their thinking around such a massive and largely abstract knowledge base. Experienced educators may find that the themes serve to re-energize thinking, introduce alternative strategies, or remind them how and why they entered the field.

Being a Work in Process

Perhaps the most significant and surprising commonality among these educators is a degree of uncertainty, of constant seeking, of realizing, as Maxine Greene puts it, that they are all pursuing something they haven't caught yet. They are more than comfortable with such uncertainty; they embrace it. Most might well characterize themselves as works in progress, still learning, still surprised, still challenged to understand and do more.

Because of their own sense of being unfinished, they also share the notion that teaching is, as Nel Nodding states, "a lifelong moral quest." Maxine Greene concurs, calling teaching "a process-oriented profession . . . helping people find their way."

Parker Palmer takes hope and confidence in his ongoing search. Looking back at his experience as a young teacher, he recalls thinking, "'After a few years pass and I get more experience, it'll no longer be so hard.' Well, I'll be 64 next year, and it's still difficult—and I mean that to be reassuring!"

Bobby Ann Starnes takes "great joy" in her belief that the quest has no end. To her, there is no final or right "it" to learn. Instead, the need to "shoot for the 'it' of the moment" keeps her work new and filled with possibilities.

By opening a window for us to their lifelong quests, these educators provide other educators support and encouragement for their own efforts to pursue something *they* haven't yet caught. It encourages them to seek deeper and deeper understanding and to find the courage to admit to themselves, and the permission to admit to others, that they are "not finished yet." As Bobby Ann Starnes points out, how could anyone not be excited about that?

The Nature of Teaching

Throughout the interviews, these educators address the nature of teaching, pointing to its complexity and the constant challenge of doing it well. Through their open discussions of their experiences as both teachers and learners, they reveal concrete examples of inevitable dilemmas faced by even the most seasoned educators and the youngest students.

The evolving, difficult, and complicated aspects of the work and lives of professional educators are revealed through intimate and rich discussions. Perhaps most revealing, they all express the power and wonder of their roles as teachers and reformers—with full knowledge of the difficulty of the roles, the lifelong quest they are on, and the enormity of changing the ways schools operate.

Throughout the interviews, the subjects reveal their understandings of and concerns about the nature of teaching. These revelations provide insights for teachers who are struggling to make meaning of the challenges and frustrations they face in their own teaching environments.

Many of those interviewed elaborate on the aspects of teaching that make teaching difficult. One of these is its very complex nature. Eleanor Duckworth understands that "... being a teacher ... is about the most complex work there is—the most physically and emotionally demanding work.... Because a mind is about as complicated a thing as there is to try to understand...."

Many recall experiences that may have seemed commonplace at the moment, but that, through reflection, were actually catalysts for a series of greater steps. As Ted Sizer says, "Most of a teacher's real 'victories' are large victories, which you believe at the time to be small victories."

Those interviewed also address the demands placed upon teachers, from both within the classroom and without. Many spoke in similar ways about what teachers must contend with in order to meet the students' needs and the demands of their teaching environments. Yet, despite recognizing the many challenges, those interviewed often comment on the pleasures of teaching, including Robert Coles. He enthuses: "It's a great job, a very special job to have that privilege to connect with young people of another generation, to connect with the future and to try to help that future become broader, richer, and stronger."

Bobby Ann Starnes agrees and shares her excitement about teaching: "In teaching, I was always trying to understand what would help learners unfold. There's no end to it, and that's a great joy for me."

It might be tempting to be intimidated by the complexities of teaching described by these experienced educators. However, beyond the personal joy one finds in teaching, there are other ways to combat the great challenges mentioned. In many cases, the respondents themselves address these issues. Several make it clear that one strategy is to make changes at one's own pace and in steps that feel comfortable and manageable. It is then important to recognize and celebrate those steps because they become the pathway for growth.

These strategies seem logical enough, but sometimes they are hard for teachers to follow when faced with an overwhelming perception of powerlessness over their learning environments. Hopefully, these and other strategies mentioned in this book will surface in the practice of teacher-readers and inspire the invention of their own strategies.

Optimism for the Future

The nature of teaching and learning defined in these interviews provides an important voice in today's reform climate. In an atmosphere dominated by scripted programs and standardized testing, these educators profess the idea that the best teaching arises out of a teacher's intellectual framework, a willingness to take risks, and the ability to remain fluid enough in response to follow the meaningful connections students make.

Although some discuss the broader educational environment as bleak, they express a kind of optimism about the possibilities for change. Ted Sizer finds optimism in the willingness to "ask the unaskable . . . say the unsayable," and believes that "question asking" leads to serious improvement in schools.

Bobby Ann Starnes also comments on the current state of education in which standardized tests and restrictive programs are too often the norm. She roots her optimism in the resiliency of teachers and their refusal to allow that "part of them that brought them to teaching . . . to be smothered. Ultimately, . . . their will, their stubbornness, . . . will take us to a different level. . . ."

The fact that teachers remain optimistic despite the challenges they face every day is astounding. What is it that keeps them coming to schools where they meet with administrators and colleagues who don't understand or support what they do in their classrooms, where their values are not shared, and where children face difficult challenges?

It is their optimism that motivates them day after day. Their optimism is often based in a belief that, through teaching, they can make a difference in the lives of young people and in their communities. Those interviewed share what keeps them optimistic despite "darker times" governing education at large. For teachers, it is important to recognize and revisit their own optimism, as well as that of the educators featured here, for rejuvenation and inspiration.

The Role of the Teacher

In diverse, yet complementary ways, those interviewed speak to the true role of the teacher and, in many cases, how they came to understand their role.

Grant Wiggins realized that a student he had at first thought of as disinterested and disengaged was very engaged in other areas of school life. He then understood that the challenge before him as a teacher was to find a way to "spark" an interest in each student.

Yetta Goodman shares her moment of enlightenment when she realized that she was a "performer and not a teacher" and determined to enter the classroom as a fellow learner in order "to create [with the students] an exciting learning experience" and environment.

Because the role of the teacher in our society is narrowly seen as that of dispenser of knowledge, teachers often find that stepping out of that perceived role is a difficult—and lonely—venture.

Robert Coles notes that, although teachers must offer instruction, they are also "moral and philosophical guides."

Yetta Goodman shares her own experience—and struggle—in dealing with a controversial political issue in the classroom. Her story about fearing the greater repercussions of talking openly and honestly about communism during the McCarthy period has a poignancy that holds true for many teachers. She discusses the lessons she learned from that experience and the ways she applied those lessons in different settings.

Understanding that these are real issues that teachers face in the classroom every day, a story like Goodman's reminds readers that these are timeless, human struggles that inspire courage by their very example.

Parker Palmer addresses our society's expectations of teachers and the "mixed messages about teachers and teaching" they receive. He points out that while we expect excellence from teachers in the classroom, "yet we

. . . devalue [our teachers]." Then "we ask them to solve all the social problems that no one knows how to solve."

Palmer's comments certainly speak to the frustration many teachers
feel when they are confronted with a society that spreads and reinforces
such messages. Knowing that Palmer and the other educational leaders
interviewed here recognize this incongruence and validate teachers' frustrations can be very empowering.

Shor and Goodman also place the role of teachers in a broader social
context. Both believe that one responsibility of teaching is to help students
foster the skills, traits, and habits necessary to become leaders and citizens
who are active participants in a democracy. This, in turn, lends to the complexity of the profession but also speaks to its remarkable weight within
the social and cultural realm.

Teachers as Activists and Agents for Change

Most of these educators see the teacher's responsibility as going beyond classroom instruction to taking on responsibility for various degrees
of change. In the midst of these statements about the central role teachers
play, Jack Shelton discusses the way teachers become the pivot point from
which educational change both originates and unfurls. While describing
the evolution of his organization, Shelton matter-of-factly states:

> We decided we should start with the people who are the most
> essential—the teachers. First of all, because we knew they were
> going to do the work, and second, because, often, the teachers
> were going to invent the work.

Shelton's way of describing the role of teachers in generating change
is different from Palmer's or Shor's in that it breathes application and strategy into the theories about *what* teachers can accomplish.

Speaking of her early career, Maxine Greene says, ". . . I believed we
could change things. . . . The ideas of being committed to something, to
move with other people even to make small transformations, are what
pulled me through to the wonderful moments."

Parker Palmer believes the seeds of activism begin when individuals
are faced with challenges that overpower some but effect energy for change
within others.

> There's something in people like Rosa Parks that—instead of
> receiving resistance as a sign of defeat . . .—internalizes that
> opposition as a sign that they are right! The problem is exactly

as big and deep and important as they thought it was—and there's something in this sort of turn of mind or alchemy of heart that takes these experiences that would otherwise be defeating and turns them into energy for change.

Ira Shor also believes in grasping this "energy for change." He calls for those "who believe in democratic education, . . . student-centered education, power sharing, and developing critical thought against the unequal status quo—we have to teach against the system, against the institution, which represents the existing authority, the inequalities . . . we're born into."

Ted Sizer advises us to "always wear bifocal glasses. . . . Look through the bottom half at your own kids. . . . But don't only do that; look up and see how [your] kids . . . fit into the larger scheme of things. . . . The way to get the changes . . . is for people who know what they're doing to take the time to look up and insist that changes be made. Those . . . are the ones who are really going to make a difference."

And Bobby Ann Starnes relates how she and another teacher saw the need to be proactive

> It was . . . about strategizing. We believed we could do more than . . . talk; we could take action. . . . We became activists for change . . . active in our local . . . organizations . . . to be . . . decision-makers. We . . . worked hard to be inside the loop. . . . It mattered because somebody was making decisions that affected our lives. . . . We needed to know who they were and . . . to influence them. We knew we couldn't just close our doors and let some mysterious others make decisions that would control and limit our teaching decisions.

The Essential Nature of Mistakes

Teachers, especially those at the beginning of their careers, worry that they will make mistakes. Yet, as these interviewees point out, it is impossible to engage in the hard work of teaching without making mistakes along the way. Because so much risk-taking is involved in improving practice and so many decisions and interpretations are made from moment to moment, mistakes are bound to be made. Starnes claims that she has made "millions," and Noddings reveals that she "still grieves over one from my first years as a math teacher." Yet while all see the mistakes as inevitable, they also see them as opportunities to understand their practice and role more clearly and to learn from each mistake.

As Vivian Paley explains, "I would say the whole point is that mistakes are essential. Study them, talk about them to the children, see if things go better when you try different things."

The Great Value of Reflection

One of the ways to turn mistakes into lessons learned is through reflection, another common theme throughout the interviews. Almost all of those interviewed talked about how important it is to, as Noddings states, "dig beneath the surface of things and mull it over, be reflective, really think about it." This kind of introspection and thoughtful assessment emerge as a significant way to address the complexities and challenges of teaching.

With the amount of pressure teachers feel to keep on a curriculum schedule and meet required mandates—which are measured so frequently by a culture of narrow testing—taking the time for reflection may feel impossible. However, the men and women here talk at great length about its rewards, its centrality in improving practice, and the various methods of reflection that may fit more appropriately within certain environments.

In some conversations, reflection is discussed in a way that simply means applying intellectual thought and rigor to ideas and practice. For example, Greene states that her thinking about her work led her to write in a more complex way that incorporated cultural perspectives that otherwise could have been overlooked.

On the other hand, reflection for some takes a form that is more concrete. For example, reflection may take the form of videography, such as it did for Wiggins, who learned a great deal about practice from watching a videotape of himself teaching. However, reflection most often is talked about as an act of writing, such as when Kohn talks about his practice of using a journal. He remarks that he dealt with both his isolation and his frustrations with teaching by keeping a journal and talking to himself about what he had written. His statement that he still draws "material from that year that has informed my thinking ever since," is a strong validation of the power of reflection.

Vivian Paley, who kept copious journals on what happened in her classroom, sees the greatest value of reflection in analyzing what went wrong. She states, "This is the great, good thing about things not going well and writing about them. Imagining doing things in another way, coming back the next day and the next week and continuing to try them another way."

Both Shor and Palmer emphasize the importance of reflection. Shor also encourages teachers to share their written reflections with other teachers and to seek a response from them. Palmer sees reflection as regenerative and as a resource for personal growth, setting "aside regular time to search my heart, in silence—walking in the woods, maybe journaling . . . whatever it is that will help me sense more clearly what's going on inside. Teachers who are in tough situations need some form of solitude to tap the wellsprings of their courage and truth."

Learning from Kids

All those interviewed talk about the great value that observing and learning from the kids they teach has on a teacher's growth. Vivian Paley tells how the learning she took from her students led to finding her role as a teacher.

> Well, as I watched and listened to the children, I saw that their sense of inventiveness was greater than mine—mine was far more ordinary, far more conventional. And I began to take the children's invented stories, either in play or in dictation, as my starting point. The degree of concentration, the degree of focusing on their part in these stories, came across to me as being filled with such passion. I knew there must be some deep reason and that I must understand it. With this understanding, my role changed to more of a connection-maker than a lecturer.

Yetta Goodman also credits her experience in observing students as initiating a turning point in her teaching practice. "I began to watch and understand kids [and] I slowly realized that even though they were responding well to me, there were kids who were not gaining a lot from the experience. I began to see that I needed to showcase the kids."

In order to deepen one's teaching practice, Donald Graves advocates that we "take the time to ask kids what their perception is of the very thing we're teaching." Grant Wiggins would agree. He believes it is a mistake to assume we understand the way students think—and the way they understand what we are teaching. He states:

> There's a door that opens into this extraordinary, strange, sobering, interesting, intriguing, thought-provoking world of, "Gee, how is it possible that the kids didn't get that? I thought they did; I thought they should have; I was so clear". . . . You should really think of the student as innocent of understanding until proven guilty by a preponderance of evidence.

Noddings, Sizer, and Coles believe strongly that teachers must know their students and something of their lives. Noddings points out that by learning what your students are "going through," you also can learn "how you can do things better." And Sizer says that "unless you know a child well, you can't teach that child very well. . . . That's why . . . I feel so strongly about getting the numbers-per-teacher down so that each child has the privilege of being known well by [the] teacher."

Robert Coles takes strength from "the privilege of learning something about their lives, learning with them about how their minds and hearts work—what they perceive to matter, what they feel matters—conversations with them, learning from them. In a sense what I try to emphasize in my books is that children (through their stories related, remembered, and conveyed) are in their own way our educators."

What's Important to Teach

These educators also talk about commonalities of progressive teaching and learning. One of the issues most often talked about was the benefits of, and the process around, relinquishing a measure of control in the classroom. For some, giving students the power of choice in the classroom became the method. Alfie Kohn talks at great length about choice in his interview. He makes a distinction between what he calls "pseudo-choice" and giving students choices that include some of the responsibilities of the teacher. He explains:

> The kids have to be able to make decisions when it matters
> very much to the teacher because that's authentic choice. We
> help kids make good choices by making sure they are informed
> about the options they have and also that the options are
> appealing. A kid who gets to choose between two workbooks
> or silly essay questions or the time of day in which to memorize
> math facts is not being offered real choice. Somewhere
> Shakespeare says there is little choice in rotten apples.

The reality, of course, is that relinquishing those choices that matter most to teachers is a frightening process. It can also feel like a distraction when so many demands are placed on teachers to prepare students for success on standardized tests. When threatened by the possibility that students may perform poorly on these tests, which also may result in a negative perception about one's teaching ability, teachers may see little benefit in taking the time to incorporate choice into the curriculum. However, allowing students authentic choice is empowering and will yield benefits that are measurable. As Eleanor Duckworth asserts, "Teachers are in a position to let kids realize the power of their minds. This is too important to let go, no matter how great the pressures are to prepare for narrow testing."

She goes on to stress that "having confidence in their own minds is a significant factor even in doing well on tests." Students learn to have confidence in their own minds when they are given authentic choices and they see their decisions respected. Allowing this to happen in the classroom can be a matter of recognizing the long-term rewards while facing the short-term risks.

For other interview subjects, relinquishing control means sacrificing the role of being the person in the classroom with all the answers and all the knowledge to impart. Maxine Greene obviously thinks this is an important point to convey to her students. She reveals, "I try to teach in such a way as to give people the feeling that I don't come in with answers to the questions, that I am as open to questioning as they, my students, are."

Allies and Community

Community and allies in the form of supportive individuals, mentors, and collective groups of like-minded colleagues, or communities in relationship to learning, were all discussed throughout the series of interviews. Parker Palmer's words embody the point each made on the subject.

> We all need community—and since community is hard to come by in this society, we need to find ways of gathering it unto ourselves. . . . Part of our task is to search out folks who are on this journey with us and gather them in various ways, creating communities that can help us follow our own lights and do the best work we can.

These interviews remind readers that others have made and are making such changes and that there are allies out there to support us when we undertake change. No one need feel they are alone when supportive communities exist or can be built.

Interviewees spoke, at length, about the importance of networking and reducing isolation. Eleanor Duckworth expresses this belief for all when she says,

> I think an important thing is to find at least one person from whom you do feel support, with whom you can talk about the things that are important to you. I think finding one person, one colleague either in your own school or in a school not too far away or on e-mail . . . I think that's very critical.

Alfie Kohn suggests that seeking this kind of support is not only helpful, but natural.

> If someone is inclined to take a chance and do something
> different—not just add some new technique like getting kids
> on the internet, but really rethinking the whole philosophy of
> learning—they shouldn't try to do it alone. They should, at
> the very least, find a colleague to supply moral support and
> new ideas to help them avoid being burned out and de-
> pressed. . . . You know, we are interdependent creatures, like
> it or not. I think we might as well like it, own it, and recognize
> that we can both provide support and derive support from
> others, even in an environment that isn't as welcoming as it
> ought to be.

Some of the interview subjects talked of using community as a way to enhance learning. Reading Noddings's discussion around communities and an ethics of care next to Shelton's, which focuses primarily on community and its role in generating meaningful learning and moral development for students, makes for a fascinating dialogue. Further, Noddings's discussion of the "dark side" of communities, meaning when they function in an exclusionary way, provides a philosophical framework for Goodman's or Starnes's experiences as members of minority communities.

As teachers face increasingly diverse classroom populations, as well as a growing movement to label and classify learners into a form of community, it seems particularly important to take into account the issues around diversity raised here. There are two contradictory trends at work in current educational thinking. First, there is a great deal of discussion around diversity and multiculturalism. At the same time, there is a significant drive toward standardization, characterized by programs that ignore populations served or site-specific concerns. Add to this environment a system of stereotyping that groups all races into individual groups, as though it would be possible to say that Black, White, Chinese, Hispanic, and other ethnic groups think, act, or behave in one way or another.

In this complex and confusing world of classrooms, teachers must seek ways to create a community of learners where the values, language, traditions, and cultural histories of their students provide common ground. As teachers ask themselves how to meet these challenges, the reflections of the interview subjects can provide powerful insights into the impact and importance of addressing the individuality of the young learners in their classrooms.

The Role of Mentors

The people interviewed also address whether they had mentors, or individuals in their lives who provided them with intellectual and professional support. Many, like Robert Coles, said that they did, in fact, have someone whom they could depend on "for their counsel, for their interpretations, for their thoughts, for their advice, for their recommendations. . . ." Some were specific individuals, while others were large groups of people. For example, Coles describes "all those school children, my teachers." While some of the mentors were famous and others occupied smaller spheres of influence, all helped these educators come into their own at different times and in important and meaningful ways.

Some mentors played the role of someone who saw great merit in their protégé's work. Eleanor Duckworth refers to Piaget and Inhelder as "intellectual giants . . . [who] cared about my work."

Others had mentors who might be seen as modeling behaviors that "showed" them things that changed their practice or thinking. Vivian Paley points to two teachers who

> . . . glowed with excitement as they watched the thinking of their students. They just wanted to know how a child thinks and were asking different sorts of questions to give the child a chance to reveal this. I learned a lot from those two people, watching them.

Bobby Ann Starnes speaks of her surprise when she learned that fellow interviewee Eleanor Duckworth wasn't certain about what she knew, that she explored her uncertainties as a means of increasing her understandings.

> She . . . let us see her confusion about a thought . . . or that she had revised her thinking as a result of conversations. . . . That had a remarkable impact on me. . . . I was able to let go of . . . the need to say something without question. Seeing that this woman . . . whom I held in such high esteem, was uncertain . . . made me feel free to do the same.

Other mentors were people who helped these educators figure out what they themselves were called to do. Parker Palmer tells us his mentor "would sit me down and help me find out what I really cared about."

Whatever the role a mentor played in an interviewee's life and career, it was seen as invaluable. Of course, these stories encourage us to seek out and find our own mentors. But perhaps just as important, they show us that we can and should be open to serving as mentors—both to students and to other teachers who seek us out.

On Being Different

Goodman and Starnes convey the childhood experiences that had powerful impacts on them both then and later as teachers. Goodman tells us of an event in her life as a bilingual minority within a system that still measures success in a way that she and her mother didn't understand. Her hurtful and potentially damaging experience suggests the need for a more inclusive culture within schools. Starnes's memory that education "was about changing me and separating me from my culture and . . . community," speaks to the same need.

The lessons Starnes derived from her experience as a minority later infiltrated her practice and helped shape her intent to "help kids celebrate who they were and use that as a foundation for being all that they might become."

Ted Sizer's years teaching in Australia brought him to a similar conclusion.

> The memorable learning was that you have to be very, very respectful and very sensitive to the values, to the attitudes, that the youngsters bring into class, that their parents have, which the community has. Ever since then, I've been loathe to say there's "one best way" to do anything, because culture and context count so much.

Connecting Experience with Practice

Throughout the interviews, revelations about early learning experiences illustrate much about their impact on the formation of educational philosophy and life mission. Those interviewed expressed their thoughts, their memories, and their experiences, sharing with readers what they underwent on the path to understanding and practicing education.

In the shape of memory, Eleanor Duckworth explains the empowered feeling of student choice in the classroom.

> . . . [One was] in my freshman year in college in a biology class. . . . I was simply to look at the bones of the leg of a horse and of a member of the cat family. And just by myself having to compare the leg bones of these two different animals and then with what I knew about my own bones was truly amazing. . . . [The teacher] gave me the opportunity to think on my own.

Donald Graves's recollection about his Spanish teacher's unusual approach to teaching a foreign language illustrates the rewards of risk-taking in the classroom.

> . . . we had a professor who wanted us to sing in Spanish, and we thought he was crazy—we could hardly make our way in this class. . . . But after a couple of catchy songs, we realized we were starting to pick up the language in ways we hadn't before. . . . It's amazing how much of a language you can learn through songs; I still have those songs with me today.

Robert Coles's powerful memory of a teacher who facilitated a personal connection between her students and Abraham Lincoln, made learning American history meaningful and played a role in his future.

> I remember her telling us about Abraham Lincoln. And then I remember seeing her crying, as did others in the class. . . . She had told us not only about someone, a president, but also about something and someone who *mattered* to her; and she had brought history alive and connected it to personal intro-spection and storytelling in a very urgent and compelling manner. The result was that I remember that moment to this day, and it was well over a half a century ago. In that moment my own working life began, because I always think of her.

Yetta Goodman, who questions the grading system in schools and makes it a practice to diminish the negative effects of grades in her class-room, reports receiving a low grade in art in second grade. When Goodman accompanied her mother, who could not speak English, to talk about the grade, the teacher told them that she gave Goodman a D because she "tried so hard. It was a 'reward'! Of course it wasn't to me. All I knew was that it was a grade that was degrading to me, and my mother thought it was ter-rible. That experience has remained with me all my life."

Jack Shelton tells about his experiences working with students in Ala-bama and his discovery that "when you see the opportunity to really apply academic skills to something, it's not abstract or meaningless but can really benefit someone. That is powerful."

Looking back at his experience in the army and how it later informed his thinking, Ted Sizer states his resulting infallible belief in the ability of people to learn. He says, "People will rise to challenges in spite of our la-beling them as 'dropouts' and non-English speakers, low testers, all of those things. Get the incentives right, get the teaching right, and almost anybody can learn anything."

When taken separately or as a whole, the interviews underscore how these educators have woven experience and practice together to determine their lives' work. Again and again, they make evident the power of the teacher to shape the classroom experiences of students. Significantly, this understanding serves both as inspiration and as a cautionary warning about the use and abuse of the position of teacher.

Conclusion

When the reader reflects on the interviews and shares the educators' memories, experiences, and ideas with colleagues, the spirit and purpose out of which the interviews were born continue. And by subsequently reflecting on one's own practice and thinking, taken-for-granted notions are challenged and one's own personal framework for teaching and learning can be redefined and revitalized.

Additionally, the interviews contribute to the greater educational conversation and put a human face and personality to the abstraction and theory that can characterize conversations of this magnitude.

Importantly, readers come away with the realization—and reassurance—that prominent educators and theorists grapple with the same issues that they do in their classrooms and in their thinking about practice. The experiences shared here and the resulting conclusions about teaching and learning that these educators have reached help to explain the evolution of a number of philosophical approaches to education.

Finally, there are stories here filled with words that inspire and hearten us during times of challenge and frustration. Maxine Greene's words are an example.

> There is nothing more fascinating . . . more life affirming, because teaching . . . is an open-ended kind of undertaking. . . . You are working with human possibility. . . . When you are a teacher, you are in a world of incompleteness . . . always reaching beyond where *you* are—the way you are helping young people reach beyond where *they* are. And that's the greatest gift that you can get. . . .

The act of reaching beyond is something teachers do every day and in every classroom. They constantly strive to reach something "they haven't caught yet" and to inspire students to reach beyond what they "caught" yesterday and today. The content of these interviews is offered in support of that act, for every day and for every classroom.

The Foxfire Core Practices

The Core Practices are the foundation of the Foxfire Approach to Teaching and Learning. They were developed by Foxfire and then tested and refined by hundreds of teachers working mostly in isolated and diverse classrooms around the country. When implemented, the Core Practices define an active, learner-centered, community-focused approach to teaching and learning.

Regardless of a teacher's experience, the school context, subject matter, or population served, the Foxfire Approach can be adapted in meaningful and substantial ways, creating learning environments that are the same but different—environments that grow out of a clearly articulated set of beliefs and, at the same time, are designed to fit the contour of the landscape in which they are grown.

Considered separately, the Core Practices include 11 tenets of effective teaching and learning, verified as successful through years of independent study. Teachers begin their work through any number of entry points or activities. The choices they make about where to begin and where to go next are influenced by individual school and community contexts, teachers' interests and skills, and learners' developmental levels.

As teachers and learners become more skilled and confident, the Core Practices provide a decision-making framework that allows teachers to tightly weave fragmented pieces of classroom life into an integrated whole. When the Core Practices are applied as *a way of thinking* rather than *a way of doing*, the complexities of teaching decisions become manageable, and one activity or new understanding leads naturally to many others.

If teachers choose the Foxfire Approach to guide their teaching decisions, it is not important where they start, only that they start. The adaptability and room for growth in skill and understanding make the Core Practices a highly effective, lifelong tool for self-reflection, assessment, and ongoing professional development.

1. The work teachers and learners do together is infused from the beginning with learner choice, design, and revision. The central focus of the work grows out of learners' interests and concerns. Most problems that arise during classroom activity are solved in collaboration with learners, and learners are supported in the development of their ability to solve problems and accept responsibility.

2. The role of the teacher is that of facilitator and collaborator. Teachers are responsible for assessing and attending to learners' developmental needs, providing guidance, identifying academic givens, monitoring each learner's academic and social growth, and leading each into new areas of understanding and competence.

3. The academic integrity of the work teachers and learners do together is clear. Mandated skills and learning expectations are identified to the class. Through collaborative planning and implementation, students engage and accomplish the mandates. In addition, activities assist learners in discovering the value and potential of the curriculum and its connections to other disciplines.

4. The work is characterized by active learning. Learners are thoughtfully engaged in the learning process, posing and solving problems, making meaning, producing products, and building understandings. Because learners engaged in these kinds of activities are risk-takers operating on the edge of their competence, the classroom environment provides an atmosphere of trust where the consequence of a mistake is the opportunity for further learning.

5. Peer teaching, small-group work, and teamwork are all consistent features of classroom activities. Every learner is not only included, but needed, and, in the end, each can identify her or his specific stamp upon the effort.

6. Connections between the classroom work, the surrounding communities, and the world beyond the community are clear. Course content is connected to the community in which the learners live. Learners' work will "bring home" larger issues by identifying attitudes about and illustrations and implications of those issues in their home communities.

7. There is an audience beyond the teacher for learner work. It may be another individual, or a small group, or the community, but it is an audience the learners want to serve or engage. The audience, in turn, affirms that the work is important, needed, and worth doing.

8. *New activities spiral gracefully out of the old, incorporating lessons learned from past experiences, building on skills and understandings that can now be amplified.* Rather than completion of a study being regarded as the conclusion of a series of activities, it is regarded as the starting point for a new series.

9. *Imagination and creativity are encouraged in the completion of learning activities.* It is the learner's freedom to express and explore, to observe and investigate, and to discover that is the basis for aesthetic experiences. These experiences provide a sense of enjoyment and satisfaction, and lead to deeper understanding and an internal thirst for knowledge.

10. *Reflection is an essential activity that takes place at key points throughout the work.* Teachers and learners engage in conscious and thoughtful consideration of the work and the process. It is this reflective activity that evokes insight and gives rise to revisions and refinements.

11. *The work teachers and learners do together includes rigorous, ongoing assessment and evaluation.* Teachers and learners employ a variety of strategies to demonstrate their mastery of teaching and learning objectives.

Foxfire Materials for Teachers

From Thinking to Doing: The Foxfire Core Practices—*"Constructing a Framework to Teach Mandates Through Experience-Based Learning"* is a book that provides a long-awaited and in-depth discussion of each Core Practice: how it is interpreted by Foxfire, the research and theory that support the Core Practices, and the ways teachers most often get started and grow in their implementation of each Core Practice. It is important reading for all who are interested in building learner-centered, community-focused classrooms.

Considering Assessment and Evaluation: A Foxfire Teacher Reader is a compilation of the most current thoughts on assessment and evaluation. The readings were selected by practicing classroom teachers from over 14,000 articles. The book includes four sections: Critical Issues, Performance-Based Assessment, Portfolio Assessment, and Scoring and Reporting. Articles include: Portfolio Assessment: Making It Work for the First Time; Grading: The Issue Is Not How But Why; What's the Difference Between Authentic and Performance Assessment?; Understanding Rubrics; What Research Tells Us About Good Assessment; and Toward Better Report Cards. Authors include: Gerald Bracey, Linda Darling-Hammond, Thomas Guskey, Alfie Kohn, Jay McTighe, Grant Wiggins, and more.

Considering Reflection: A Foxfire Teacher Reader is a wonderful compilation of articles that will support all teachers who wish to strengthen reflection in their own classrooms and in their own personal practice. Also included is a bibliography and Foxfire reflection materials.

Considering Imagination and Creativity: A Foxfire Teacher Reader brings together discussions on the significance of imagination, creativity, and the aesthetic experience in learning. Through these readings, strong arguments are made that creativity and imagination have implications far beyond the arts and that, in fact, all learners need these traits in order to make meaning of their school and other learning experiences.

The Foxfire Magazine has been in continuous production since it was founded in 1966, and its basics remain unchanged: meeting curriculum mandates, students helping to make decisions, and the recording and preservation of the Appalachian culture, heritage, and rapidly disappearing dialect. Two issues per year are published, featuring personalities, history, and how-to articles from Appalachia, written by Rabun County High School students.

These books and magazine, as well as books in *The Foxfire Book* series and additional Foxfire publications and products, may be ordered by phone, fax, e-mail, or website via the following:

The Foxfire Fund, Inc., P.O. Box 541, Mountain City, GA 30562-0541,
(706) 746-5828 phone, (706) 746-5829 fax,
foxfire@foxfire.org, www.foxfire.org

Sara Day Hatton has worked as a writer, editor, jeweler, communications specialist, adult education teacher, and newspaper reporter. She derives great pleasure from being with family and friends and spending as much time outdoors as possible. A graduate of Appalachian State University, she lives in the mountains of Western North Carolina with her husband, David, an arborist.